THE LEMONADE STAND ON THE CORNER

HOW TO START A SUCCESSFUL BUSINESS AFTER 50

VICTOR BENOUN

THE LEMONADE STAND ON THE CORNER

HOW TO START A SUCCESSFUL BUSINESS AFTER 50

VICTOR BENOUN

W Business Books

an imprint of New Win Publishing
a division of Academic Learning Company, LLC

ISBN 10: 0-8329-5018-1

ISBN 13: 978-0-8329-5018-6

Manufactured in the United States of America

12 11 10 09 08   1 2 3 4 5

Library of Congress Cataloging-in-Publication Data

Benoun, Victor.

The lemonade stand on the corner : how to start a successful business after 50 / Victor Benoun.

p. cm.

Includes index.

ISBN 978-0-8329-5018-6 (hardcover)

1. New business enterprises--Management. 2. Small business--Management. 3. Older people--Employment. I. Title.

HD62.5.B463 2008

658.1'10846--dc22

2008028791

CONTENT

The significance of the baby-boomer generation in the business world. Sharing my story. Making the decision to become an entrepreneur. Understanding the difference between a small business and a personal business. The importance of passion for what you do. Determining your compelling reason for starting a company.

Declaring your desire for success. Practice and pretend you are successful. Using imagination and visualization. Discovering what you would do if your knew you could not fail. Goal-setting versus resolutions. Listing your top 100 goals for your life. Measuring success.

Learning your strengths. Understanding what you like and dislike in business. Describing your personality. Seeing opportunities everywhere. Finding a niche. Filling voids due to outsourcing. Specialization. Transferring skills. Networking. Your sphere of influence. Viral marketing.

Your attitude. The law of expectation. Finding opportunities everywhere. Partnering in business. Franchising. Licensing. Manufacturing. Naming your company.

ACKNOWLEDGEMENTS

I am very grateful to Arthur Chou, Michael Harris, and everyone at WBusiness Books. Besides being a class act, you are visionaries and understand how to make dreams a reality. Thank you for your help and support.

To my wife Anngel, who has inspired me for 28 years.

My thanks goes to Eddie Conner, who suggested I write this book in the first place. You are an amazing human being and make the world a better place by being here.

To Cynthia Richmond, you are a great friend. Thank you for everything you taught me.

Mari Florence, you are an unsung hero. I wish you great things in life.

To Nick Mirras, Chuck Evans and David Hall, thank you each for your friendship for the past 25 years and unwavering support.

My deep appreciation also goes to John Paul DeJoria, Rick Wetzel, Veronica Judish, Paul and Julia Provost, Amanda Stone, Cheryl Gocke,

ACKNOWLEDGEMENTS

Charlie Yacoobian, Lee Salz, Bruce Anthony, Laina Sullivan, Nancy Tierney, Rob Deigh, Willy and Robyn Spizman, Henry DeVries, David Reff, Michael Schur, Diane Kane, Judi Irwin, Jeff Lewis, Dinah Eng, Ron and Arlene Gold, Sue Bernstein, Mike and Mira Armstrong, Eddie and Laurie Hallman, Aaron and Lisa Henderson, Randy Lane, Nancy Giltner Maher, Robert Rosenthal, Patti Heckman, and Lynne Visciglia. Thank you!

To my family, Sam and Jean Benoun, George and Lillian Yacoobian, Joel and Jennifer Sherwin, thank you for the examples you left for me to follow, as well as your love and your support. Thank you to Glenn, Rachel, Andrew and Evan. Also to Sammy, Yogi, Morgan and Murphy, you've given more than I can ever give back.

To my clients past and present thank you for allowing me the honor to work with you and do what I love.

INTRODUCTION

If you are over 50 and out of work, you're probably experiencing one of many emotions right now. It depends largely on *why* you are out of work and whose decision it was. If it was yours, and you have been thinking and planning on breaking away from your daily routine to become the entrepreneur you were born to be, then congratulations, your time is now! If, on the other hand, your former employer made the decision *for you*, then you are probably not experiencing a blissful moment at this time.

Look, it doesn't really matter how you got here; you *are* here! So now you must deal with that. The good news is that there is plenty of support for you. There are more opportunities than ever to become self-employed. You can be a one-man shop working out of a space in your home or build an entire empire stretching out over thousands of square feet of commercial space; the choice is yours. According to the AARP, Americans 50 years of age and older account for 40% of all self-employed people.

Turning 50 can be tough enough emotionally for many of us, because we feel like such a large part of our lives is over. Toss in the challenge of building a new career and becoming self-employed, and we can become overwhelmed! But it doesn't have to be that way. You have a choice in the matter. You also probably know a lot more than you give yourself credit for, and, believe it or not, your thrust into the world of entrepreneurship can actually be a blessing in disguise.

Think back to when you were just a kid. Perhaps you set up one yourself, or maybe you just spent your allowance there, but we're all familiar with "the lemonade stand on the corner," that early burst of entrepreneurial energy that so clearly defines the American spirit.

As quaint as it might seem, the lemonade stand showed you everything you needed to know about business—how to pick the best location, paint an attractive sign, prepare a fresh product, and serve it with grace and style. Back then, packaging yourself and your product was the key to your success, and the constant threat of the kid down the street kept you on your haunches.

Unfortunately, after most of us grew up and found our place in the job market, those humble beginnings at that corner stand were soon forgotten. Fast-forward now to 2008, and we find fewer jobs, fewer companies in the United States, and sparse opportunities for business as usual. The future of the employment market is uncertain. As difficult as it seems to accept, corporations today have gotten used to working with less—less staff, less money, *less you.*

Yet difficult times also bring opportunity. You just have to know where to look. It doesn't matter what your political background is or whether you believe America is headed in the right direction or not—because those things ultimately don't matter. The market does not make us; *we make the market!* According to a 2003 report in *The Atlanta Journal-Constitution,* more than 3 million jobs have already left the United States and many more are on their way out. We must face the reality that these jobs may never come back.

After the introduction of *"the new economy"* of e-commerce in the 1990s, the world has gotten smaller due to globalization, and competition has become fiercer as a result. Job security has become a thing of the past, as more companies make the decision to outsource their services to take advantage of cheaper alternatives to homegrown domestic experience.

Some displaced workers will venture into entrepreneurship because they are done with the daily routine of the nine-to-five part of their lives and are looking for something more. They are also seeking something that fits in better with their lifestyle at their present age or with the lifestyle they hope to have. Others will opt for early retirement and will want to take advantage of the financial independence they've achieved, knowing they have the security of their pension or other retirement benefits. If they had forethought early on and were able to plan, they have years of savings to fall back on should something go wrong. Then there are those who have no choice in the matter—those who are 50 years of age or older and now labeled an undesirable hire despite their years of experience, who seek entrepreneurship out of necessity.

Here's the reality: It's not unusual for employers to want to hire younger workers for their company—recent graduates who can be molded as management desires and who, of course, will work for less money. Is this a case of age discrimination? Perhaps. But when a perspective employer is interviewing candidates, the young man or woman often has a leg up on the competition even though he or she lacks the experience of those who have already "paid their dues," so to speak. Here's an important question: Are companies getting the same results with younger workers that they once received with more seasoned workers? A better question might be: Do they care?

The good news for the older unemployed crowd is that they can start their own businesses and be wildly successful. According to the AARP, people in their mid-50s through their mid-60s are the ones most apt to create their own companies and work for themselves. Is it hard work? Yes, it can be; but didn't they already work hard for someone else?

Today's workforce is going through an incredible upheaval—a renaissance, to be more precise. But change is only as good as the energy you put into it. If you sit back and watch, life decisions that you may not ultimately be happy with will be *made for you*. However, if you embrace change with both arms and eyes wide open, you're likely to end up with a result to your liking.

As the saying goes, "If life gives you lemons, make lemonade." I've also heard, "If life gives you lemons, throw them back!" Just because someone tells you what you can do, doesn't mean you have to listen. Live life on *your* terms, not someone else's. If not now, *when?*

IT'S TIME

There's no way around it, we must recognize the fact that the business world is very different today than it was just a few years ago. There is no such thing as job security. You probably already know this. In fact, downsizing is the buzzword of the moment and has been for years. How many people do you know who are out of work or looking for a new job because their salary/hours/benefits/overtime/bonus has been cut? Do you know anyone who fits that description *intimately?* Corporate America is rapidly becoming an unfriendly environment for Joe and Jill Citizen, especially those within the over-50 crowd—those smart, well-educated, hardworking folks who just want to be fairly compensated for their day's work and years of experience.

Under increasing pressure from shareholders who want to see bigger and quicker yields on their investments, companies are now largely driven by the bottom line: profits. The result is that, in order to justify their existence, companies have shown little mercy, sacrificing you, the employee, in order to display a better bottom line for shareholders and investors. Banks and savings and loans have joined one another or have been gobbled up by competitors. Tech companies have merged; the media is now run by just a few conglomerates, and other big employers have just plain shut down, moved, or outsourced operations to Canada, Mexico, or India, to name but a few.

So, what if you are one of those affected by this unyielding trend? Are you fearful of ending up as a statistic? If you answered "yes," then you're not alone. And if you've picked up this book, you already have an inkling that you need to make some serious changes to your life. I'm here to help.

If you are in the over-50 category, here is perhaps the toughest part: For several years you may have worked in a corporate environment with massive structure, layers of management, and excessive rules and regulations. So now, you are breaking free from the corporate lifestyle that has occupied your mind for as many years as you've been in the workforce. You will probably have to change some of your work habits to be successful as an entrepreneur. If you are not a self-starter, you will need to become one. If you are used to waiting for instruction, you are now the instructor.

You are the creator of your destiny from this point forward. People don't change overnight. Believe me; *I know*! You have been molded to think as corporate policy dictates, but as an entrepreneur, you will become the master mold maker. It can be a bit daunting, scary, challenging, and exciting all at the same time. Remember, though, you are molding your future as *you* see it and desire it to be.

I don't deny that what you will experience on the inside will be unsettling. But an entrepreneur over 50 years of age has the benefit and experience of all those working years, as if he or she were learning while someone else footed the bill. Now you can apply everything you've learned and create your business *your way*.

In reality, what you are about to do is as hard as starting a lemonade stand on the corner. All you need is the desire, the right ingredients, and the knowledge to put them together. You provide the first two, and I'll chip in the know-how.

Let's get started.

CHAPTER 1
BACK TO THE BASICS: THE LEMONADE STAND FOR ADULTS

The journey of 1,000 miles begins with one step.
– Lao Tzu

Congratulations! If you are over 50 years old, you have been granted automatic entry into an exclusive club, known as the *Baby Boomer generation*. Our generation has witnessed some of the greatest achievements in history, including space walks, heart transplants, and the creation of the transistor radio and the portable television.

We have left our footprint on society. You can turn on your radio today and hear music that was recorded 40 to 50 years ago by Elvis Presley, The Beatles, The Rolling Stones, Bob Dylan, and Tina Turner, to name but a few of the artists.

Cable television is still populated with programs that were hits when I was growing up. "The Adventures of Ozzie and Harriet," "I Love Lucy," "Gilligan's Island," and "The Wild, Wild West" are still on channels across the country and probably across the globe throughout the day due to the popularity they had and still have.

Hollywood caters to us and has made recent movies based on the cartoon, "Underdog." "Batman" has turned into a movie franchise and introduced to a whole new, younger audience today, based on the success of the '60s television show. "Zorro" has had two successful installments on the big screen, as a result of the Walt Disney television show.

We are a talented, resilient generation, capable of accomplishing great things when we put our minds to it. Entrepreneurship happens to be one of those things we need to turn our attention to.

Working hard and being diligent comes with our territory. That's why when we are faced with adversity, we respond to the challenge and accomplish our goal. This book is about providing you with the information you need in an easy-to-understand manner so you can accomplish that goal. We must be doing something right because there are more than 1 million new companies started each year by the Baby Boomer generation, according to the AARP.

MY STORY

I began working in the lending industry a year out of college and loved it immediately. After a few years, I was specializing in real-estate finance. I realized, however, that I had become bored and disenchanted with the company I worked for due to internal politics and the bureaucracy with management. No matter what caused my discontent, I wasn't happy and I eventually left the company and moved to a new one.

During that time the economy suffered through recession, stagflation and deflation, and then, at times, it prospered and boomed. These cycles were nothing new to me.

I worked for four different companies in a 12-year time span and was getting ready to move again. However, I couldn't help but feel that switching employers again was not going to be the answer I was looking for, nor would it make me any happier or satisfy me. I had to face the facts.

In my case, the last thing I wanted was my own business. While I considered it from time to time, I quickly convinced myself that I wasn't smart enough, didn't know enough, and wasn't in touch with the right people. It eventually became crystal clear that I had no choice in the matter. I was miserable where I worked and the realization hit me that moving to another company was only going to be more of the same. I was very frustrated by the status quo. If I wanted to remain in the mortgage industry, I could no longer put off the inevitable.

I really didn't know any more about running my own company than I had known before, but now I had the desire, which is the life force of any business—the water, if you will. Whatever I didn't know, I would learn. If I didn't know what licensing was required, what legal or accounting work had to be done, others did. I wasn't reinventing the wheel. "Other people have done this," I told myself. All I had to do was seek out those who had already been successful and who knew how to do it.

THE ESSENCE OF THE RECIPE (IT'S MY SECRET, BUT THIS ONE YOU CAN SHARE!)

In many respects, successful businesses today are fashioned from something nostalgic—something old-fashioned and familiar. When you are hungry, for example, which do you prefer: a fast-food apple pie or a fresh, hot apple pie that has been made by hand with care and love? Would you prefer a pie that has been mass-produced and merely reheated for whoever happens to be next in line at the drive-through? Or would you prefer a piping-hot, just-out-of-the-oven pie that was made with you in mind—with just the right amount of spices and cinnamon dusted on top?

I'm not knocking the Golden Arches, but I know what I prefer. If I have a choice, I don't just want pie, I want fresh, hot apple pie, with apples picked from the backyard apple tree. If you are over 50, then you probably remember the character Aunt Bea from *The Andy Griffith Show*. She was always making pies from scratch for her family. Even though it was only a television show, I can actually imagine how Aunt Bea's pies must have tasted, and how I would like pie to taste when I make or order it.

Sometimes as a culture, we are so used to being told what we can have that we stop thinking about what we really want. If we want to save time, then we go through the drive-through and get as close to what we want as is available. Here's where the role of the entrepreneur enters: discovering what people want, what others are not doing, and then creating and delivering it in a highly accessible manner at an affordable price.

If you think closely about the companies that have been major successes with their customers, they all share one underlying quality: valuing the customer above all, and making sure their products and services are proof of this. IBM, General Motors, and General Mills are just a few of the companies that have succeeded for decades because they always put the customer first. After all, if you don't have customers, how do you have a business? I don't need to sell you on starting your own business. You're already here and you're looking for the secrets to success. What I'm about to share with you are the secrets for growing a successful business, one that thrives as a result of the personal attention it gives its clients.

A PERSONAL BUSINESS

Understanding the answer to one simple question will land you squarely on the road to business from the get-go and set you apart from other companies. The question is: **What's the difference between a small business and a personal business?** Technically speaking, a small business is one that is comprised of 500 employees or fewer, according to the Small Business Administration (SBA). However, in today's world, a small business simply provides goods and services—a cold exchange, the way most businesses operate. A small business is a way to make *your* ends meet as a business owner. But a *personal business* is so much more than that. It is a business that works diligently to ensure its clients' needs are met with the utmost care and individual attention on an ongoing basis...for life! The fact that you are over 50 affords you the excellent opportunity to take care of your clients better than anyone else because you have years of business experience and you know how to make a measurable difference in the lives of those with whom you do business. Everything you do and desire to do is related to better ways of serving your clientele.

A personal business is one that "clicks" with its customers and goes beyond a traditional business relationship. Borrowers with whom I have worked in the past don't hesitate to call me to ask any number of questions, because they trust me. Their queries range from my opinion on purchasing a new car to insurance questions, or even to discuss career paths. Sometimes the questions are even real-estate related.

Don't make the mistake of not taking the time to talk with someone when they call, even though they are not buying something at that time. I've heard stories about many younger entrepreneurs and salespeople not spending time on people unless those individuals are there to purchase their goods or services. The last thing you want is for one of your customers to call someone else. They are already comfortable with you and value your opinion and thoughts; otherwise they wouldn't be calling. This is a little something extra you can do to show people how much you value them.

DANCE, DANCE, DANCE

There is a line from the movie *Flashdance* theme song that goes "take your passion and make it happen," which goes to show that you can find sage advice in the strangest of places. This particular bit of wisdom you can apply anywhere in life you please. What is passion? It is the fire alive in all of us, pushing us to follow a course that will bring an outcome of overwhelming satisfaction. Not following your passion leaves you with an emptiness and hollowness that eats away at you and leaves you with a hunger to fulfill your innermost desires. It is nature's way of telling you that you need to turn your attention to the path that you know in your heart you should be following.

Passion is an essential element of starting up a personal business; it can even be the difference between success and failure. There will be long days and even longer nights when you first set sail on your own. A rose garden, it won't always be; but with passion, it will become your life's mission. Passion will bring you to what you were born to do. Passion brings purpose to your mission so that you create a unique experience for your public and satisfy your desire through entrepreneurship. When you are doing what you love— your life's work—you can see that it is anything but just a job!

There is a saying in sports, football in particular, that goes "Leave it all on the field." It's a saying that is applicable to life and everything that we do. It means, give all you have to whatever you do, whether you are running for touchdowns or creating marketing plans. Give it every ounce of your energy, your sweat, your desire, your passion, your enthusiasm, and your breath. Don't go back to the locker room with any untapped potential. It won't do you any good to save it. The same can be said about life, and any aspect of it. When you are so committed to something, anything, there is no way you can fail. Mistakes will be made, of course, but mistakes are a far cry from failure.

Failure is not taking the initiative to do the things you want to do to be joyous. It's not taking the time to strive for success. Mistakes are just the residue of being alive. Only two types of people don't make mistakes: liars and those lying six feet under.

Success is also a lifelong quest. If you have some good fortune with your hard work but allow complacency to enter, or you ignore current business trends and growth, you will eventually have problems. On the other hand, when you embrace what you love and make it a reality, it will bring you success, but it won't feel like work. You will reap the rewards that spring from creating something from nothing, and you will experience the joy of watching it grow into something magnificent.

Now in all honesty, self-employment may not be for everyone. It's like home ownership, or having a puppy; it may just not be for everyone. There are careful considerations to be made, as well as hard work and commitment day-in and day-out. If you are willing to make that commitment, you will most likely attain a level of satisfaction reserved for the few who are willing to put themselves on the line to follow a dream and create the life they want. These are people who want to discover just how good they are at what they do. These are people who are not satisfied with anything less than their best performance. And, they want to know they lived the way that Dr. Wayne Dyer so aptly described: having not "died with their music still inside them." These people will never say, "I should have, but I didn't."

NO PAIN, NO GAIN

There is no question an element of risk exists when you are opening your personal business. I think there is a difference between taking a chance and taking a calculated risk. If you do your homework in advance, you will discover that difference between the two. Besides, it cannot be assumed that risks don't already exist when you work for someone else. There are no guarantees in life. There are no assurances you are safe at your present job. Just ask the people at Enron, WorldCom, or the country's former largest sub-prime lender New Century. These companies, as well as others, serve as ghastly proof that even in this day and age, people must be prepared and equipped to take care of themselves and be responsible for their own futures. Personally, I *encourage* it.

Since questionable accounting practices have come into play, more and more companies are subjected to having their books challenged. How many more Enrons are lying dormant? Besides, no one says you have to quit your present job cold turkey and start working full-time for yourself. Start slowly, part-time if you want, and build from there.

If you make the decision to open your own lemonade stand, be sure that you have a thorough understanding of your own *compelling* reason for doing so. Determine the most self-satisfying work you can do, and don't just go where you can earn the most money. Making money is certainly a wonderful thing, but the problem with money alone as motivation is that you are only serving *your* needs, and not the needs of your clients. You are looking at the picture from the standpoint only of what's in it for you. You are dooming yourself right off the bat.

To succeed, you must be "client driven." That means you must ask how you can serve your clients better than they are currently being served. As Donny Deutsch, advertising guru and television show host says, "There's gotta be a better way." It's fair to assume that if you are experiencing problems with some facet of life, and existing products and services are still not satisfying your needs, then you are probably not alone. It's a good bet that other people are experiencing the same frustration and lack of satisfaction that you are. Take a look around you and see what might need fixing or improving. By solving a problem for the public, you will undoubtedly prosper in the process.

In my case, I had often heard how frustrating borrowing money to buy or refinance a home could be. Oftentimes it seemed that the whole process was just plain mysterious to consumers. Despite the best intentions of all parties, transactions always seemed to have surprises, which led to their cancellation. Someone who wanted to couldn't sell his home and someone else couldn't buy the home he wanted, which ultimately resulted in a lot of wasted time, money, and effort.

I took inventory of my work history, and created a résumé complete with all my accomplishments. Along the way in my career, I had worked for three Fortune 100 lending institutions and a small mortgage banker. Each had its merits as well as disadvantages. I thought how effective I might be if I could take only the best resources and experiences from each of the lenders with whom I had worked, and pass those onto my clients so I could offer the best lending experience possible. I discovered that the idea had merit.

You can be the best at what you do as long as you care enough to bring the best of all your experience to the table. I knew that in order to be successful, I would have to have a clear understanding of *why* I was doing what I was doing. In reality, the last thing the world needed was another mortgage company.

How about you? Do you know what motivates and drives you to succeed in this world? For instance, do we really need another computer technician, inventor, or restauranteur? Most likely, the answer is no. But then we come back to that argument for having a compelling reason, desire, or passion for accomplishing anything. While the world doesn't need just another technician, it *does* need a technician who can give the public the care, service, assistance as only you can. The world needs a restaurant that offers unique recipes, incredible values, and a place to gather with family and friends. Let's sum it up this way: The world needs *you*!

I don't think any two people see things exactly the same way; there is always some subtle nuance. This allows you to conduct business exactly as you see fit, and as a result, exactly as your customer will appreciate. We crave people who satisfy not just our needs, but also our wants, giving old-fashioned hands-on service while using the technology and tools of today.

ON-THE-JOB TRAINING

If you are currently working for someone else, maybe a large corporation or company, you have the unique opportunity to build your business while someone else pays for it. It's up to you to realize the opportunity before you. At the same time, it's also up to you to provide your best efforts and produce results you will be proud of when you work for someone else. First of all, you are being paid to utilize your skills and talent in whatever your field, so you always want to do the best job you are capable of doing. Otherwise, you won't be paid for very long.

Second, you may be placed in contact with people who could wind up being your future clients. You never know. Think of this also as building your personal network. Networking is establishing contacts with people outside your normal circle of influence, including individuals of different backgrounds and occupations. When I started with my first savings and loan in 1983, I was actually shaping my own personal business for years to come. I wasn't aware of it at the time, but by working hard for my clients, I was building a long-term association with both buyers and Realtors.

Since I worked for a large company, people didn't tend to call specifically for me. However, I ended up getting their calls because of the geographic area I handled. Eventually, it wasn't the savings and loan that became the responsible party in the mind of the client. Instead, it was I. Looking back, I certainly see how well the experience served me.

My point is, just because your name isn't on the door doesn't mean your attention and best efforts are not required. You may have a chance to achieve something unique, to meet or assist people; don't let it get away. Additionally, many companies offer employees the opportunity to finish school or get an MBA. They offer training, seminars, and possible advancement. Appreciate the options before you, and make the most of them.

Something to be mindful of is the fact that many companies are aware of the identities of the highest performers at their competitors' companies. They know where the talent lies and how deep it runs. There is nothing like getting phone calls from the competition trying to romance you away by offering you a better or varied experience as well as more money. Here is the point to remember: The world is a much smaller place than it used to be. You never know with whom you may want to work, who will want to work with you, and from where future clients may come. You *are* your personal business. Use your talents wisely.

LEMONADE-STAND INGREDIENTS

Complete an assessment of your core values. You are driven by your values in everything you do. Take a look at the following list and pick five values that you feel drive your behavior. Rate each of them on a 1–10 scale, with 1 having the highest priority and 10 having the lowest. Then, on a separate sheet of paper, write a brief reason why each one is of importance to you. Not everyone will choose the values that you do. Your choices will help give you a clearer understanding of the things that truly matter to you and will serve as a guide in your quest for entrepreneurship.

1. Love	**8.** Fairness	**15.** Friendship
2. Integrity	**9.** Passion	**16.** Influence
3. Family	**10.** Responsibility	**17.** Joy
4. Peace	**11.** Trustworthiness	**18.** Wisdom
5. Success	**12.** Power	**19.** Health
6. Recognition	**13.** Happiness	**20.** Trust
7. Caring	**14.** Wealth	**21.** Competence

CHAPTER 2
DREAMING BIG: REDISCOVERING YOUR LEMONADE STAND

Setting goals is the first step in turning the invisible into the visible.
   – Tony Robbins

I've learned along the way that in business, as well as in life, there are no rules as to who is allowed to be successful and who is not. It is not dictated by education, race, or sex. Instead, it is more likely determined by your own driving force. Sure, it's easy to say that the more you have riding on your side perhaps the fewer obstacles you will face, but there are no guarantees. History is full of examples of people who came from humble backgrounds yet who eventually overcame the odds in their quest for success. At the same time, we hear about many who, despite coming from privileged backgrounds, wallow in mediocrity and discontent.

Success comes in all colors, races, and ages. According to an article in *USA Today*, 5.6 million workers over the age of 50 are self-employed. That is an increase from 1990 of 23%. *USA Today* reports that those numbers will increase over the coming years as baby boomers look to *themselves* for job protection, as opposed to the corporate world.

The United States government reports there are approximately 25 million non-farm small businesses (you already know I prefer the term *personal business*) throughout the country. In fact, 58% of the workforce is comprised of small businesses, which means that they employ an estimated 55 million people. These same small businesses create over three-quarters of all new jobs in America; and women-owned businesses account for 3.5 million alone. You should also know that many entrepreneurs end up with failing ventures due to poor planning. According to a study published by the University of California:

- 50% of all new businesses fail in the first five years

- Only 20% will survive in excess of 10 years

- Half of those that survive are barely profitable

This is a reality of entrepreneurship. There are no assurances that an education from a major university will ensure happiness, success and riches. There is also no guarantee that a life beginning in poverty and seemingly without opportunities will banish you from your wildest dreams. Perhaps being born as you were provides the stimulus to seek your life's ambition, but you must have a goal, something to which you aspire.

We are often afraid to discover what we are capable of; in our minds, doing so can be dangerous. As children, we were encouraged to play, dream, and pretend. But then the deeper we dove into academics, the further removed we became from those dreams.

Ask a child what he or she wants to be in life, and sit back and enjoy, because the sky is the limit. Anything is possible to a child. When we get older and alas, more responsible, we soon forget about those fun-filled days. Regrettably, most students are not taught how to "think outside the box" in our schools. Instead, many are taught how to memorize information and pass tests, how to climb the corporate ladder and get a good job—usually working for someone else.

I don't intend for this to sound mean-spirited, but in many respects, our teachers and parents don't serve as the best role models because they often perpetuate the image that being self-reliant isn't necessarily a virtue. In fact, according to their beliefs, it can be reckless. How many of our parents fall into the same trap: going to a job, day-in and day-out that they despise, caught in a rut from they will never break free? I was fortunate that my father had his own desire to break away from his daily routine, and have his own lemonade stand on the corner. I didn't realize it then, nor did I appreciate, but the apple didn't fall that far from the tree.

So how do we learn to go for our dreams? We start with our own innermost desires and work outward. We then declare them. I have attended seminars where attendees break down into small groups, and one by one, each declares his dream as if it has already happened.

For example, one person said, "I have just won the Academy Award for the movie I wrote the score for." Someone else said, "My paintings just fetched the largest price in history." Another said, "I am slim and trim now because I exercise daily."

Then the members of the group, declare back to each individual his or her dream: "You have just won the Academy Award, congratulations on your success." "Your paintings are fabulous; you deserve to receive the money for these wonderful paintings, as they bring pleasure to others." And finally, "You look fantastic since you started your exercise program. My butt looks so big next to yours." And yes, that was actually said!

You get the idea. Each person had a different reaction to the experience. Some were truly uncomfortable publicly declaring their dreams and receiving accolades and praise—as if they didn't deserve it. But that was the point of the exercise: to acknowledge that each person is worthy of the success they seek and to make certain that each and every person is comfortable with that potential success, no matter what their dream.

You don't have to attend a seminar to do this. You can instead gather some friends together and share each other's desire to accomplish something big. Just take turns declaring what you want to do. Then allow the group to give you the positive feedback you deserve, and do the same for everyone else.

If you feel like you are on a desert island, are embarrassed, afraid, or don't feel supported, you can still do this on your own. Go out and get a tape recorder and declare your own intentions for yourself. Give yourself the feedback you desire to hear. You may want to do this, regardless. There is something very powerful about hearing your own voice encouraging you and rooting you on.

If you are considering skipping this exercise or think it is silly, think about this: The subconscious mind cannot distinguish between what is real and what is imagined. So why not imagine yourself accomplishing your wildest dreams? The more you hear it, the more likely you are to believe it. Whether your goal consists of going to the moon, climbing Everest, or being the next Bill Gates or Steven Spielberg, it all starts with a vision, a dream. Make yours count.

As I said, some people were uncomfortable discussing their dreams during the seminar. Unfortunately, we get used to repressing our own creativity and desires, so when opportunity arises, we don't always know what to do. We feel embarrassed or egotistical, as if we are not entitled to live the life we desire. We feel shame that others might think we are unworthy. Whatever else you do, don't forget this point: **We spend far too much time worrying about what others might think!**

Try this on for size: Write about yourself in the third person, so you can feel more objective in declaring your success.

"John has written the novel of the century."

"Pat has discovered a cure for cancer."

"Tony has discovered an exercise that everyone loves doing."

Close your eyes. Visualize yourself in your greatest moment, in a scene, doing what it is that you want to do. Experience everything as it happens. Both mentally and physically experience the sensation; feel what it is like to be what you want to be. The more energy and passion you pour into it, the more real it will feel.

Speak aloud, as if you are being interviewed on radio or television.

Recount how you accomplished your goal with ease. Have fun when you practice and pretend. The key words are *practice* and *pretend*.

At this point, I'm using examples that don't necessarily focus on entrepreneurship in order to simply familiarize you with this exercise. It can be a little intimidating if you are not used to pretending and dreaming and then pressuring yourself to decide what you want to do with yourself for the rest of your life. This can be complicated, especially if you were forced into leaving your former company.

Make-believe is not just for youngsters. Even at 50+ years of age, we can still be young at heart and most certainly want to be. Life is much more fun when we are not always so serious. A light heart and a sense of humor are great tools to have as we each build our own lemonade stands.

Now let's apply the above exercise to our personal businesses. Not sure what you want to do? Well, in what areas do you already shine? You can transfer your accomplishments and skills to a new occupation.

When I opened The Mortgage Source, Inc., it was easy to pretend I was helping people attain the great American Dream of home ownership because I had done it previously for years. Though I knew nothing about renting an office space and purchasing a phone system or an office copier, I visualized it as a smooth and easy experience. It turned out to be exactly that, because I had no reason to think to the contrary. Besides, I was so miserable at my current job, anything would have been better than staying at that company.

Now it's your turn. Get out some paper and a pen and answer the following questions:

1. What would you do with your life if you knew success were guaranteed? Think about it. Dream big. Now close your eyes and visualize what your life is like doing what you would like to do, experiencing lasting and satisfying success.

2. To what would you dedicate your life if you *knew* you would succeed? Is there a special cause that you would spend your life supporting? Would you save the whales, save the ocean, help cure cancer, or make

life easier for seniors?

3. What kind of contribution would you make to society? Imagine what the world would be like if you did work that came from your heart, brought you ultimate enjoyment and satisfaction, and benefited everyone in the process.

4. What kind of difference would that make? When you see the world in your mind's eye, what does it look like to fulfill your innermost dreams? Are you making it a better place? Are you opening doors for others? Have you fulfilled you own curiosity and intellectual growth beyond your own belief?

Begin writing, and try to feel what this would be like so that you really experience it. Your feelings are very important in this exercise. Even though we are discussing business, realize we are a *feeling* society, and not one driven solely by how we think. You must honor both your head and your heart, if you are going to be happy and successful. Are you a bit excited as you start this? I hope so. This is the first step toward embarking upon a new journey in life, and one of the most difficult parts is writing down what is important to you.

Are you smiling as you become more aware of the choices open to you? Are you maybe even chomping at the bit to get started? *Good!* If you experience your dream and how it feels in your imagination first, and then write about it on paper and describe it, it is ultimately much more likely to materialize in your life.

GOAL-SETTING

I can remember as a child writing my goals down on paper and then crossing them off my list as they were accomplished. Then new goals took their place, and so on. That was the problem. It seemed like it was more important to cross them off the list without really savoring them and *enjoying* the experience. It was like a checklist: "I've done this and I've done this...OK, let's add some more now." In many respects, it was more important to finish the task than to enjoy the journey.

Now, more than ever your goals serve as compelling reasons to guide your life. Evaluate what you want to accomplish. It might be that you want to have your company operational in 30 days, to earn $1 million in one year, to retire in 10—whatever is compelling for you. It is important that whatever you decide to accomplish are *your* goals, and not someone else's. If they are not yours, you will be hard-pressed to follow them.

Now, write down everything that is of interest to you: all your goals, everything you want to accomplish in your life. Don't evaluate anything that you write, just *write*. If anything doesn't feel true to you, then it may mean it is not really your goal.

This exercise alone could take several days. The more you get into the groove of dreaming, the more you will want to add. Keep your list handy, and as you weigh and consider options, be sure to keep a record of them. Remember, our lives are in perpetual motion, and your needs and desires will grow and change constantly.

Goal-setting is an easy way to evaluate where you are and where you want to be. You will see that goals differ from resolutions—those usually made around the beginning of each new year. Goals are ever-present and ongoing, while resolutions come around once a year and then seem to quietly disappear a few weeks later. Unfortunately, our resolutions may not be as urgent as we think they are. If they were, we wouldn't wait 365 days to make them.

Some sample life goals might be to:

1. Write a best-selling novel

2. Enjoy a home on the beach

3. Bicycle across the country

4. Meet the President of the United States

5. Make a million dollars

6. Learn to paint

7. Take up yoga

8. Make a million dollars in the next five years

9. Learn to play bridge

10. Win a poker tournament

11. Become a mentor to someone

12. Act in a movie

13. Perform on stage

14. Learn to sing

15. Become a photographer

16. Go on a safari

17. Visit an exotic location

18. Teach a class

19. Run a marathon

20. Donate money to charity

You might make a list of 100 or more goals that are important to you to accomplish before you die. The reason I want you to do to this is to appreciate what you want your lifestyle to be as you get ready to open your own company. Incorporate your life goals into whatever your chosen endeavor might be. While completing this exercise, as well as all the others in this book, you are going to begin to get an inkling of the life you want that incorporates not just how you make a living, but all the elements that go into leading a complete life.

SHARE THE MOMENT

There is nothing like sharing your dream with someone you care about. If you have a significant other, include that person in your vision. Support from someone whom you care about and who cares about you is invaluable.

No matter how driven you are, how lucid your plans seem, there are bound to be a few days where things don't go exactly as planned. Having someone to confide in will be appreciated. There will also be times filled with grand excitement and accomplishment. To share those with loved ones and friends is exhilarating.

If you have a family and are responsible for putting food on the table, the more support you have from them, the better. Also, when you are first establishing your personal business, you are likely to have some long hours. Part of it is necessity while part is excitement and exhilaration because you *want* to do it. Those long hours might be part of your business, so keep your friends and family involved in what you are doing.

MEASURING SUCCESS

Once you determine what type of business you want to have, you will no doubt envision yourself as successful. Here's an important question for you: How do you measure success? If you don't know the answer, how will you ever know if you are successful? After all, if you can't define success or measure it, how will you recognize it when it arrives?

Therein lies the problem, and the secret as well. Success means different things to different people. If success is measured in monetary terms, then how much do you need to make, and over what period of time? Does being a millionaire equal success? Is that a likely goal based on the personal business you plan to establish? If you can't celebrate until the goal is achieved, then what will keep you going until it is reached?

Personally, I think it is easier and more pleasurable to enjoy small victories along the way to lifelong goals. For example, the first time to feel good about what you are doing is as soon as you take some action toward your goal. It might be conducting research, doing some planning, or scheduling a meeting—whatever it is that takes you one step closer to what you want. Don't just think about what you want, *do* something about it! By taking that first step, you've done more than most, and that's what separates you from being simply a dreamer.

There is no question in my mind that success means being able to spend my life doing what I enjoy while earning a living. If I can go through life helping others to achieve their dreams, then I'll be a happy guy. I also know that money will only motivate me so far. Yes, money is important and can bring lots of fun, but I know I must receive a level of satisfaction and fulfillment or I won't be happy. To me, having a personal business is all about being happy. You know when you've helped someone and when you have really earned the money you've made. There is no feeling like it in the world. You don't have to say a word to anyone; the smile on your face tells all.

Now it's your turn. It's time to go into the kitchen, cut up some lemons, squeeze them into a glass, add some water and just a little sugar (*real* sugar, not that "sweetener" stuff), and enjoy a glass of delicious homemade lemonade. Because now I'm going to help you build your own lemonade stand on the corner.

LEMONADE-STAND INGREDIENTS

On a sheet of paper, answer the following questions:

1. What did you want to be when you grew up as a child?

2. What would you like to be known as your greatest achievement?

3. What is your idea of success?

4. Do you have a role model? If so, who and why?

CHAPTER 3
PERSONAL INVENTORY: THE FOUNDATION OF YOUR LEMONADE STAND

Too many of us are not living our dreams because we are living our fears.
    – Les Brown

So, what is your compelling reason for having your own lemonade stand? Were you one of the unfortunate ones pushed out of a comfy office and forced to fend for yourself? Or will you virtually explode if you are kept from going after and achieving your potential? At the same time, are you a little afraid? Perhaps even scared? Bordering on terrified? That's all right; there is no shame in that. The only shame would be spending your life only thinking about what you *might have* become, but were too frozen with fear to take the first step.

I will make this easier for you so that you can walk into any situation you want and already possess the confidence and strengths you desire. In essence, it's time to take inventory of your strong points—literally.

Let's go back to the piece of paper on which you were listing your goals. What do you bring to the table? By that, I mean what do you recognize (and others recognize) as your strengths? What is your burning desire? How can you leave your mark on the world and make it a better place? Remember, your idea doesn't have to be original. Like I stated earlier, the last thing the world needed when I started out was another mortgage company. Yet opening The Mortgage Source, Inc., provided me with the opportunity to do real-estate finance, *my way*. As Frank Sinatra sang, "I did it my way."

Sit down in a quiet place where you will not be disturbed. Turn off the television, phone, pager, computer, whatever; you need some time to yourself. Now start writing. Ask yourself these questions:

1. **What can you offer the public that no one else can?** This can be anything from where your professional interests lie to what you are good at and enjoy doing. Remember to include the most important ingredient in your answer. Don't know what that is? The answer is obvious, of course—**YOU!** Don't laugh. When I did my market research, I asked some trusted Realtors for their opinion. Most responded, "I don't know where you work now; I just call **you**."

   I received plenty of input from others too. The company didn't matter; they just wanted to work with me. I had to be sure that once my personal business opened that I could deliver the goods to get the job done, but the first step was accomplished and a big question was answered. **People trusted me**. No matter what you promise, at however great a price, if you don't have the trust of your clients, then it won't matter.

   If you are fortunate enough to have an existing clientele, and you are able to gain insight and input from them, then you are certainly at an advantage. However, before you talk to anyone, use your judgment and determine if it is appropriate to discuss something like this with him or her. It may or may *not* be, depending upon your relationship. Use care in your decision. It may be wiser if you talk to family and friends instead.

   Now, go back to your paper.

2. **What do you enjoy doing?** By this I'm asking you not to identify a career, but rather what makes you *happy*. We'll have plenty of time to

think about what type of business you are going to establish. Right now, let's only consider the types of things that should be included in your company. Down the line you will be able to identify a career, but that comes later. On a scale of 1 to 10, with 1 being least desirable and 10 being highly desirable, rate the following:

1. Working with people

2. Working behind the scenes

3. Using your hands to create

4. Using your imagination

5. Handling rejection

6. Refusing rejection

7. Negotiating

8. Keeping your word

9. Accepting responsibility

10. Getting the job done no matter what

11. Being a self-starter

12. Staying motivated

13. Working independently

14. Thriving on challenges

How would you describe your personality? Are you afraid to commit and make a decision? Do you get emotional over everything? Are you flexible? Do you stick to your guns no matter what? (In other words, are you stubborn?) There are no right and no wrong answers. The information you have written will be useful to you in understanding which areas you wish to embrace and which you choose to avoid.

You may already have a specific idea or career that you would like to pursue. If you haven't chosen a specific industry, does a field already exist in which you could involve yourself and eventually improve? Do you understand the guts of computers and possess the skills to create or improve hardware? Do you have the verbal skills to communicate with others, whether orally or in written form? Do you understand blueprints? Do you know how to build homes, design shopping centers, teach children, or discover vaccines? Can you make the best doughnut in town? Can you read tax returns or understand investing and planning for retirement?

What pushes your buttons? Do you make a great sandwich? Can you create an iced tea that quenches the driest thirst? Or, do you have the knack of making people laugh or cry with joy with the greeting cards you write, design, and create?

You are becoming an entrepreneur because you want to do things *your* way. You want to make your own rules, and be your own boss. (In reality, your clients are your bosses, because they will ultimately rate you on how you are doing.) You want to do what you do because of the joy it brings you.

As you consider your options, remember that opportunities are everywhere. What do you see when you watch television, read a newspaper, look in your closet, or open your garage?

The home-fitness craze developed out of the growing number of people who desired to go to the gym and work out, but had neither the time nor the money to do so. It is now a multibillion-dollar industry, and new products are being added, subtracted, and revamped almost daily. Is there something you could add to the mix?

Do you get lost easily? Look at the GPS industry and how it has developed personal portable-GPS systems. It's bad enough getting lost in your own town, what about when you go to a new city and have no idea where the heck you are? Ever try reading a map at 65 miles an hour in an unfamiliar area? If you've missed as many turnoffs and on-ramps as I have, then you definitely know the value of a GPS system. Now they are available not only for cars and bikes, but there are also hand-held models available for hikers. Directions can even be delivered to your cell phone. What a country!

I remember the first time I saw an extensive takeout-food counter with hot prepared meals at the supermarket. At first I thought how nice it was that our local market did this. Later I found out that this little convenience—having dinners ready to go that you could pick up on your way home—was over a $3 billion business per year. I had no idea!

Take that one step further, and look at the companies that deliver meals to your home daily; it's almost like having a personal chef. Someone who recognized a glaring hole in our society is filling it and getting paid handsomely in the process. Can you do the same?

Look what Starbucks and Seattle's Best have done for coffee. It wasn't long ago that a cup of coffee cost anywhere from 10 to 50 cents. Now the price for just a plain cup of coffee approaches and sometimes exceeds $2.00. Now consider the price of some of the fancy bar drinks that cost upwards of $4.00. Get the idea? If you do, you too can revolutionize an industry, and in most cases, have a line of people waiting to purchase your product.

The fact of the matter is, it's not just about drinking coffee; it's about the *experience* of coffee. Starbucks is only one of several coffee houses that have comfortable chairs, soothing music playing in the background, and tempting desserts in its display cases. Offering an alternative to clubs and bars, it's a great place for people to meet, relax, and enjoy themselves. People gladly pay for that enjoyment.

We haven't spoken yet about e-commerce and businesses on the Web, but I want to share with you a story I read. It was about a young man, 18 years of age, as I recall, who loved to go fishing. It was what he lived for; all he wanted to do was fish. He took his love of this sport and built an inexpensive Web site and began selling every type of fishing lure available. *Fishing Lures*!

The site became so successful that after only a year or so, he was offered $1 million for his business...an 18-year-old kid! The only difference between him and someone else is that he took what he loved and did something with it. That is so important.

With that being said, let's go back to your list:

1. Since we've been talking a lot about using your imagination and visualization, what can you see yourself doing on a daily basis for the next several years?

2. Does this business concept open the door for spin-off products and services? For example, if you are selling air-conditioning systems, can you offer a service policy to inspect and change the filter every six months? If you install windows, can you offer a service to clean them every quarter? If you are a landscaper, can you offer weekly service to insure the yard looks as good as when you designed it? If you sell fishing lures on the Internet, can you also offer fishing poles, tackle boxes, fishing hats, and other clothing items?

3. How does your business concept relate to your core values? Do you believe in what you are doing? Does it fit in well with your family and lifestyle?

4. Consider what you already know how to do as an option. Does it translate to a personal business or is it limited by design?

5. Is there some occupation or service that has been outsourced to some other country that now leaves a gaping hole for someone at home to fill? You don't have to have a large office space with tons of square footage in order to be effective. Most likely, only a small office space is needed, and for anything else you need, you can turn to places like FedEx-Kinko's, Staples, and Office Depot for the business specifics that you need. You don't have to have an office full of equipment and hundreds of people working at your company to make it a successful one.

6. Is there a niche you can fill? By that, I mean can you specialize? In the mortgage industry, for example, you can try to do it all, or you can specialize in what are termed 1 to 4 units, also referred to as single family residences. Some companies may offer only apartment loans, while others provide loans for commercial shopping centers. You may enjoy working with first-time home-buyers, or on the other end of the spectrum, working with seniors by providing reverse mortgages. You can create a diet program for the masses or a diet program for nurses. You

might be better off leaving general subjects to others and instead, becoming a specialist in one area.

7. Is there something that you have always wanted to do? Nothing says you can't take your passion (there's the word again) for cooking, designing, building, freezing, manufacturing, sewing, or something like that, and build it into a business.

I saw an interview with Rachel Ray, the daytime-talk-show cooking diva, who said she didn't have formal training in cooking. It's just something she always enjoyed. She learned how to do it, and now she has her own show on network television, her own magazines, cookbooks, as well as merchandise bearing her name and likeness. She freely admits she is not a *chef*, yet because she loves food and cooking, she has become famous for her abilities in the kitchen.

What was your occupation with your previous employer? Can that be adapted to a personal business? For example, if you worked in a large insurance company, can you offer insurance services to individuals or to business? Can you become a consultant in the insurance industry or an expert witness in the legal profession? If you worked in a bank, can you offer financial services, help people plan for retirement, or invest in savings instruments? If you worked behind the scenes in television, can you teach others how to edit film, work a camera, operate sound equipment, or start up their own production company?

If you are still not sure of what you would like to do, drive up and down the streets of your neighborhood and notice what kind of businesses are in operation. Are you familiar with them, meaning, do you already do business with or buy from them? If you do, is there something you can do to improve the services they offer?

You can pick up the Yellow Pages, look through any category you want and explore what appeals to you. From A to Z you can go through page after page and pick a business for yourself that would really get you excited. In the process, think about how your life goals can be worked into your lifestyle.

NETWORKING

The reason we are broaching this subject here is because networking can be essential to your success in many ways. The concept of networking is to establish strong personal and business connections. Like anything else, it requires time, work, and energy to be successful. Building a deep pool for social networking and even business purposes requires your efforts to work for the mutual benefit of all parties. It's not all about *you*!

As indicated above, networking can be for personal or business reasons; both types have benefits. Your friends and family, per se, constitute one type of network. It is probably a very casual and informal one, but it gives you the ability to be yourself and have others see you that way. It is easy to discuss hot topics in the current environment with them and to talk about and listen to conversations about things in our society that are working, as well as those that aren't. Somewhere in that conversation might be an idea on which you can capitalize.

If you listen carefully to what people say, you can pick up ideas about what pains them and what is missing from their lives. This opens a door for you to find a mutually beneficial way of solving that pain.

Think about it for a second; when you seek advice on personal matters, you may speak with those in your social and family network. If you want information on what's happening in the employment market and what gaps need to be filled, you turn to your business network. It would make sense then that they can aid you as you develop your business plan. You can get a variety of opinions and information that can be vital to the establishment of your business and its success. In essence, you can gain feedback and then conduct market research to see if your business idea is a sound one.

Another important reason for networks is that they can work for you, just as you can work for them. If someone asks you if you know someone who can fix a widget, and someone from your network actually *can*, you are going to refer him or her. In the same respect, your network is going to spread your name among people they know as well. One of the first questions raised when someone starts a new company is, "Where will my business come from?" If it is a traditional brick-and-mortar company, often the first clients come by way of referral. In many respects, the same can be said if your venture is on the Internet.

So is there a way your network can more effectively "help" your company? Yes there is. It's based on the concept of the **sphere of influence**. The sphere of influence is based on the idea that everyone knows 250 people. Now you may not think you know that many people personally, but on average, that is how many people you will eventually know. Perhaps there are people you haven't seen or spoken to lately, but you still know them.

Now, start making a list of everyone you know. (You can tell I'm big on lists—that's because they work!) Begin with family and friends. Include their names, addresses, phone numbers, e-mail addresses, cell phone numbers, Web sites, and blog addresses if applicable. Move on to include business associates, doctors, dentists, dry cleaners, teachers, administrators, carpet cleaners—anyone you can think of. When you are done, peruse the Yellow Pages and look at the different occupations and industries. See if there is anyone who you can think of that you know for each category. Afterward, go through the White Pages, look through the alphabet and search for any familiar last names you may have forgotten. You are going to want to keep all this in some type of data-management system, because this list will become an integral part of your success down the road. One thing to keep in mind is that the people in your sphere of influence will continue to grow, and the quality of your list will continuously improve—meaning that the more successful you become, the greater your referral sources.

In his book *The Referral of a Lifetime*, Tim Templeton suggests that if you know 250 people, it's safe to assume that they also know 250 people in their sphere of influence. That's 62,500 potential referrals. Tim says it's not only whom you know, but also whom your friends and clients know. Think about it for a second: If you had 62,500 clients, would you even think twice about being successful? You can see how the power of leveraged marketing can work for you.

How do you get e-mail addresses and cell phone numbers if you don't have them? As you move closer to opening your business, I suggest that you send out a letter to everyone whose address you do have telling them about the opening of your forthcoming company. You may offer them discount coupons or other offers in exchange for them completing a questionnaire providing the address information you want. Additionally, ask about their personal well-being. I always want to know what my friends and clients are doing in the business world because I want to be able to refer them to others, as well as receive their referrals. You will be doing both of you a favor.

There is no substitute for a strong database. In fact, there is a saying in business that goes, "he or she with the best database wins." It's true. It doesn't matter how good you are or how good your product or service is; if no one knows about it, it doesn't matter.

Want to build client loyalty? Refer your friends and clients as often as they refer you. Whenever I call a client and tell them I am giving their name and number to another of my clients, they are absolutely thrilled to be valued that way. Think about it this way: In order for us to be successful, our clients must be successful. Otherwise, they won't need or be able to afford our services.

Every year I send a new questionnaire out so I can update my database. People move, change jobs, have children, and so forth. Basically, their needs are always changing. If you are aware of these needs, you can better serve them and, at the same time, understand how they can also serve others in your database. Your goal is to be the first one your clients think of when they or someone in their sphere of influence needs what you do.

VIRAL MARKETING

Sounds like a disease doesn't it? "I have a bad case of viral marketing." Henry DeVries of the New Client Marketing Institute (www.newclientmarketing.com), a faculty member at University of California San Diego Extended Studies and coauthor of the book *Pain-Killer Marketing*, defines viral marketing as "word-of-mouth advertising meets the Internet." He explains that the goal is to get other people to mention your business name and note how great you are on various Internet sites. Once you have determined the nature of your business and have established a Web site, you can begin your own viral-marketing campaign. You need not have already opened the doors to your business, as this campaign will help inform the public that you are coming.

"Content is king on your site," notes Henry. "Make sure you give something away of value whether it be in the form of special reports or informative articles, e-books, or other interesting information. Give it away for free." Henry also suggests optimizing search engines and contributing articles to other sites because they will always mention your name and usually, your site as well. E-zines (online magazines) are always looking for content, and even though you may not receive monetary compensation for your contributions, you will be promoting yourself for free. According to Henry, "They will almost always put a blurb at the end of the articles that mentions you as the author, and often, a link to your Web site." In addition, Henry recommends contacting various organizations and offering to be a speaker at one of their events. You should record such lectures when possible.

"Utilize sites such as YouTube, Craigslist, and MySpace. Get people talking about you," suggests Henry. He also acknowledges that time is a limited resource and many baby boomers may not have the techno know-how to be effective online. "In that case, hire a college student or ask around. There are plenty of people who know what they are doing and will work inexpensively just for the opportunity to build their portfolio." He advises that you find similar businesses to your own and see what they are doing online so you know what the competition is doing. "If they have a place for comments or a blog, you may even be able to leave a comment. Always be polite. And due to the law of reciprocation, a competitor may even link back to your site," says Henry.

LEMONADE-STAND INGREDIENTS

On a separate sheet of paper, answer the following questions:

1. What is your greatest strength or asset?

2. Why do you feel this way?

3. What is your biggest weakness?

4. Will this deter you or interfere with what you want to accomplish?

5. Is there an existing idea or product that you can change today to improve it? What is it, and what would you do?

CHAPTER 4
ALL SHAPES AND SIZES: CUSTOMIZING YOUR LEMONADE STAND

I have always been driven to buck the system, to innovate, to take things beyond where they have been.
— **Sam Walton**

Anything is possible with proper vision and attitude. Just ask the Wright Brothers about their invention of the airplane or Dr. Robert Jarvik about his invention of the artificial heart. Our outlook is extremely important in everything we do. I'll give you a few examples.

I read a story about a shoe company that was based here in the United States, and like any good business, they were looking for ways to increase sales and expand their company. Eventually, they looked to the Continent of Africa as a potential market into which they could move. After all, it was a vast area with a large population.

The story goes that the sales manager sent two salespeople to different areas to scour the countryside and determine what they could learn about the potential to grow a company like theirs in Africa. After two weeks, the first salesman phoned his home office. Dejected and worn down, the first salesman told his boss that he was looking forward to returning home as soon as possible. He explained that the last two weeks had been a complete waste of time and money; as he put it, "You see, no one here wears shoes."

Just a few hours later, the second salesman called his manager with great excitement and enthusiasm. "Boss, Boss!" he began. "We've got to get started right away! We have an incredible opportunity to help people here; you see, no one here has shoes."

When you recount the story from both parties, it is the same thing, isn't it? It just depends on how you choose to see it. The first salesman saw no value in what he did or how he could help people, based on how things had always been done before. The second salesman had the vision to see what the future could hold in Africa if he helped everyone who currently didn't have shoes. He saw a golden opportunity to improve many lives.

Another concept I read about has to do with what's called "The Law of Expectation." In simple terms, it means you get what you expect. It explains how someone who thinks he is sick can actually be cured by taking a placebo—a sugar pill. The person doesn't know the placebo is not real medicine, and thus expects the pill to cure what ails him. So for him, it does.

The story itself is about a group of school children, along with their parents and teachers, who were told that those who did well on a test demonstrated excellence in academics. In reality, the exam could determine no such thing. At the end of one year, those in the group that was told they had done well on the test showed a significant rise in IQ. Again, you get what you expect.

Is there a way to get what you want and expect without playing tricks on yourself and instead, taking a more direct approach? There absolutely is. You set a deliberate intention; you *decide*. The dictionary defines the word *decide* as follows: "To settle conclusively all contentions or uncertainty. To make up one's mind. To come to a conclusion. To cut off from all else. To select a course of action and cut off all other possibilities."

As you begin your journey as an entrepreneur, think of times in your life when you experienced absolute success. Focus on that and ignore any problems you experience along the way. Recreate the mindset you had then as you approach every task and challenge before you. Once you decide that you are going to create your dream business, you are well on your way to having it.

The more specific and determined you are, the better. If you are still not sure at this point what you would like to do, then let's look at some other options, perhaps some things that you might want to consider.

TO PARTNER OR NOT TO PARTNER (THAT IS THE QUESTION!)

There is a lot to consider when entering into a partnership with someone. In many respects, a partnership is like a marriage. While getting along isn't a prerequisite, because you spend so much time with this person, it's certainly a preference.

How would you judge your own temperament? Are you capable of doing everything that needs to be done, physically, emotionally, and financially? If not, you may want to work with someone else. There are definitely pros and cons to establishing a partnership with someone. A partner offers an opportunity to share responsibility as well as liability. It also provides someone to bounce ideas and strategies off of and someone with whom to resolve issues.

Having a 50-50 partnership also means that someone else has an equal say in what goes on in the company. To some extent, this will be determined by how things are structured. I considered working with a partner when I opened my own lemonade stand, but ultimately chose to go it alone. There is no right or wrong; it just comes down to your individual preference for the type of venture you wish to open.

You can have more than one partner; in fact, you can have many. Law firms, for example, often have multiple partners. Because he wanted to share responsibilities as well as financial obligations, my accountant Michael has a partner. David, another Certified Public Accountant (CPA) I know that works in my office building, said he planned to start slowly. He wanted to grow the business himself and didn't want input from anyone else. He apprenticed with a Big Eight accounting firm, learning his industry over the course of time and doing things his way.

You might specialize in one service or offering, and your partner may bring a different strength to the table. Combined, you can be an awesome pair. If you do indeed choose to work with a partner, have a *partnership agreement* written by an impartial third party to protect everyone's interests. A partnership agreement spells out the percentage of ownership of each partner as well as his or her individual responsibilities. It should also include an exit clause should one partner decide to leave the business, or happen to die. Don't be embarrassed or afraid to discuss a partnership agreement. Utilizing such an important tool does *not* mean you don't trust your partner. You wouldn't go into business with that person if there existed a lack of trust. It is easier to discuss this agreement in the beginning, when there are no problems or misunderstandings.

FRANCHISES

Don't have a clue what you want to do in life other that the fact you want to work for yourself? Nothing says you have to *know* a business to be in business. Many people with a desire to start a company consider purchasing a franchise. In fact, people 50 and over are the largest segment of the population investing in franchises today. This is due to the fact that many baby boomers leave their former employers with a golden parachute—enough money to live comfortably—but are not ready to retire. Others have saved money all their lives and now is the time they want to use it. Still others, who may not have been blessed with either of the above, may have equity in their homes that they can borrow against in order to start a franchise.

Laina Sullivan (lainasul@gmail.com) has been involved in the franchise industry for 25 years and, in the process, has worked for some of the largest success stories in history. She helped franchise Supercuts, Penguin's Place Frozen Yogurt, Gloria Marshall Fitness Salons, iSold It, and Easyriders. It's easy to understand why I wanted to speak with her when it comes to franchises.

Laina says that 900 new concepts for franchises were introduced in the past three years. Prices start as low as $50,000 and go up to $900,000 for some of the new opportunities. "When considering a franchise, many people think only of McDonald's, Burger King, or Domino's Pizza. Maybe that's how it was a few years ago, but not today." She goes on to explain that in many cases, businesses can be run right out of a home or small office space. You don't need a lot of square footage with a big overhead and staff.

Some of the areas which are booming now are: home health care, accounting and tax service, auto and truck rental, dating services, financial services, fitness-training services, florist shops, snack services, restaurants, hair salons, real-estate services, security and locksmith services, closet organizers, home inspection services, dry cleaning, carpet and upholstery cleaning, duct cleaning, lube and oil centers, curtain and mini-blind installation services, and consultants in almost any industry including corporate cost reduction. In fact, almost anything you find in the Yellow Pages probably has a franchise opportunity.

When you purchase a franchise, you are supplied with everything you need, from training to staffing, purchasing, advertising, newsletters, and district-manager assistance. The support you receive from the corporate office is not free. In addition to the franchise fee you pay, there are monthly royalty fees, which are based on a percentage of sales.

So how do you recognize the next big thing? The first thing Laina suggests is to take a personality test in order to determine what you enjoy doing and where your strengths lie. She then recommends purchasing a copy of *Entrepreneur Franchise 500*. It's published once a year and profiles all different industries. She also suggests you acquire a copy of *The Franchise Handbook*, which is published twice a year, and subscribe to *The Franchise Times*, which is published monthly. You may additionally want to consider attending the annual franchise convention in Las Vegas.

Like everything else we are talking about, this is all about doing your homework. However, Laina stresses that you don't have to be experienced in a particular field to become successful. In fact, she says that's one of the reasons you are purchasing a franchise in the first place: so the corporate office can train you.

Many people stepping out of a corporate environment for the first time are concerned about how they are going to manage without someone looking over their shoulder. Again, Laina says that's part of what you are paying for. Franchises have a formula for success. If you can follow directions and aren't trying to reinvent the wheel, then you should acquire the success you desire.

Corporate offices want you to prosper because you become a profit center for them as well as for yourself. But this also benefits you. That's because the consumer knows what to expect, wherever in the country, or world for that matter, he may be. In exchange for all you do, the corporate office heads do all they can to ensure your success.

The important thing is, if you are considering this avenue and are able to afford the franchise and monthly royalty fees, then you may be in an excellent position to attain your dream. In purchasing a franchise, capitalization is an important factor. You can be denied the opportunity to purchase a franchise if the parent company believes you don't have enough backing. This may apply to you if you're working out of a spare bedroom in a residence or office. Not having enough funds to weather the storm can plunge a stake into the heart of your plans.

Laina recommends that you visit the corporate office and observe what you can. There are a few warning signs, in her opinion, of which you should take note. For example:

- Is the training room nicely furnished and set up for presentations, or is it empty? If it isn't being used regularly, looks like it is collecting dust, or it's being used as a storage room, there could be a problem.

- Are the salespersons pushy? If it seems like they are more concerned with their welfare than they are with yours, then that could be a sign of a larger problem. They may be starved for cash flow or could be closing down franchises. The purchase of a franchise is supposed to be for the mutual benefit of all parties.

- Are they too eager to get your money? This is another sign they may be in trouble. If you feel that you are being rushed into signing or contributing funds, then you want to take a step back to examine what is really happening.

- Do they encourage or discourage you from speaking to other franchise owners? Other franchise owners should be their best source of advertising. When a franchisee is satisfied, he tells you and encourages you as well.

- Are many stores being closed or relocated? If stores are closing, then it may be a sign that the franchise is not working. You want to know if this is a limited situation or a company-wide trend.

- Does the corporate office own any of the franchise stores? If a franchise is such a good investment, then the corporate office would likely own some. If they *do* own corporate stores, how many? If they don't, then why not?

FRANCHISE YOU

Let's say you have a unique idea for a product or service. Can someone purchase your franchise? The idea is for you to sell your expertise as well as your name in exchange for a fee. Now you may not be McDonald's, but perhaps your name lends credence and creates value for someone. If this is indeed the case, it represents an opportunity for you to make money. Laina says this happens all the time. It's as simple as having a good idea. However, franchises are tightly controlled, and the legal fees and paperwork are extensive. It doesn't happen overnight.

You have to file a Uniform Franchise Offering Circular (UFOC), which is one of the documents you get before you franchise. It includes a list of suppliers, background on principals and staff members, an operating manual, a table of contents, a cost breakdown, the number of open stores, advertising fees, franchise and royalty fees, and a list of franchises currently operated by individuals, as well as store-owned, closed, and relocated franchises. It is a lot of work, and you will inherit a pretty hefty legal bill when you are finished, because franchising is tightly regulated.

I could sell a franchise to someone wanting to get started in the mortgage business and provide that individual with everything they need. It's not something in which I have an interest, but it is certainly another way to generate income.

A college student who wanted to make and sell a better sandwich than those he found near college campuses created Subway. Despite its humble beginnings, Subway has now become a major franchise across the country and beyond. This is an example of someone who started with a single idea and pushed it forward. If you have an idea for a better smoothie, sandwich, bookstore, taco bar—whatever, take a look at the potential of your idea and how it might translate to multiple locations.

Colonel Sanders made a very good living in his senior years by selling fried chicken. Yet before he ever had his first franchise, he gave his recipe to various restaurants in exchange for a commission for each dinner sold. He knew his recipe was different and unique enough to help sell more chicken, and he was proven right. In essence, before there was ever a Kentucky Fried Chicken restaurant, he franchised his recipe. Do you have an idea that can be franchised?

LICENSING

Licensing is a way of using someone else's design and placing it on your product to create value. For example, cartoon characters, music groups, sex symbols, and even the likenesses of wrestling superstars are made available in exchange for a fee. They can be found on everything from T-shirts to underwear. You pay a fee for this, but it adds a perceived value to what you are offering and can make the difference of your product being seen as unique and desired by the public, and therefore, salable.

In the same respect, can you create something that others will want to license? It may be an idea for a character, a product name, a drink, or a new food creation. In turn, companies would pay you a fee to license your creation and put its likeness on their product for the purpose of attracting or increasing sales.

My brother-in-law, Charlie Yacoobian, is currently co-owner of a company called Racebricks (www.racebricks.com). His company licenses cars as well as the likeness of NASCAR® drivers for his product. He offers the following advice to those who are considering getting a license. "Many of the companies want large dollars up front. There is no guarantee as to what will sell or what will not, so don't be overly aggressive, especially when you are starting out." He notes that there are different licenses for different products, so the cost of a license for a T-shirt can be different than the cost of a license for a purse, children's bed sheets, or lunch boxes.

Charlie points out that you must be well-capitalized. It can take up to a year to obtain a license. He said that for NASCAR®, he had to submit a business plan, a product prototype, a marketing plan, artwork, as well as a final sample. All this can take time, and then when the finished product is ready, you have to worry about knockoffs. As you can see, there is a lot more here than you may initially have thought. Obviously, licenses are acquired all the time, and in his case, it made the difference between having a product to sell and *not* having one. He started selling his product online and then eventually moved into retail stores. The one suggestion he has for someone new in business is to take a beginner's bookkeeping class.

BRING IT TO MARKET

Maybe when it comes to creating a product or niche, you are entrepreneurially challenged. Perhaps you are a real misfit. Fine. Find someone else's product or service and inquire how you can exclusively represent it as an agent and collect a commission. Get the exclusive rights to distribute and build a nationwide network. Sounds like a good idea, doesn't it?

My friend Nick Mirras is a real genius. He is amazingly talented and creative and has many great ideas. However, he maintains a full-time job, so he doesn't have the time to invest in taking his creations beyond the beginning stage.

Nick showed me a prototype he created for one of his ideas: The 13 Hour Clock. It's a novelty item for people who don't have enough time in the day. The hours run 1–13 as opposed to 1–12. The face of the clock says,

"What do you mean there aren't enough hours in the day?"

Nick had gone to a discount store and purchased a nine-inch-diameter plastic clock, took off the plastic encasing, popped out the dial and the face, inserted the new face he'd made on his computer, refastened the hands, replaced the plastic casing, and for about $4.00, had his prototype. I thought this was really smart thinking on his part and a truly fun idea. I asked Nick what his intention was for the product and what he planned to do with it. He had many big ideas, but unfortunately little time. I asked him how he felt about having a partner so the product could be brought to market. He replied without hesitation, "Yes."

That was good news and bad news. At the time, I had no idea how I was going to do this, but through a series of introductions, I met Bruce Anthony (banthony1991@hotmail.com) who helped me find an overseas manufacturer. I then sold a large number of units to a major catalog company. It was a lot of work, and I learned a great deal in the process. It was really a hoot though, when I viewed the completed product—the culmination of a lot of hard work.

Bruce is a manufacturing facilitator, with 33 years in shepherding overseas manufacturing. He worked for Weider, a fitness-equipment manufacturer, for 17 years, and during that time, established associations with many other fine manufacturers. He notes that manufacturing is still done here in the United States, especially for plastic products, but the cost of labor for many products has become cost-prohibitive. Bruce echoes a familiar theme, "Move cautiously and do your homework. There are many good companies out there, and unfortunately, many that are not so good." When you search the Internet for overseas manufacturers, you are never really sure if you are looking at a manufacturer or an agent. These are the types of things that add cost to your product. The best way to find a good manufacturer is to ask around and attend trade shows and gift shows.

Now, one thing to be mindful of is, once a product is manufactured overseas, it still has to get *here*. What is the method of shipping offered, how much will it cost, and what will that add to the cost of your product? You also have to write to the Department of Customs and get a *ruling* on your product. You will have to pay a duty or charge for your product to be allowed into the country. This will also add to the cost of your product.

In your search, you may look for new businesses that have not been marketed properly—or at all, for that matter. Attend trade shows and seminars. Look through newspapers and the Yellow Pages for ideas. If something is marketed or sold locally, then investigate widening the target market. This might involve opening other locations or starting up an online business. You must find some way of using your ingenuity to reach new clients.

IMPROVE AN EXISTING IDEA

Research existing businesses and companies that are of interest to you. Can you improve an existing concept? You might find that you can become a business consultant to a specific industry. I'll give you an example: I'll never understand why movie theaters are run the way that they are. Everyone wants to go to the movies on the weekend. How many times have you tried to go out on a Friday or Saturday, or even a Sunday, only to find that tickets for the movie you want to see are already sold out? It's happened to me several times over a lifetime. Now you can buy tickets online and in advance, but that still means that a certain number of people are not going to get a seat. Ever been to a movie on a weeknight? More often than not, you can shoot a canon through the theater and not hit a soul. Why not offer discounted tickets for primetime movies during the week and fill the place up? It sure seems like a logical plan to me! If I had an ownership interest in the movie business, I would offer primetime movies at half the price and then distribute coupons throughout the neighborhood to let the community know about it. If I were a business consultant, I would go to theaters and observe their attendance during the week, during the afternoons, on weekend days and nights. I would then write a proposal on how movie theatres can increase revenues. As a business owner, you have to pay rent and salaries and all the other expenses whether the place is full or empty, so why not get some butts in the seats? Even 50% of something is a whole lot better than 100% of nothing.

Success in business is all about discovering new ideas or improving existing ones. Don't be shy; your opinion is important. What qualifies you to be an expert? Well, you are a consumer; you go to the store, attend movies, buy clothing, shop online, eat at restaurants, travel, stay in hotels, fly on airplanes, and go to sporting events. Have you ever been approached by someone who asks you to complete a marketing survey or to be part of a focus group? These are ways that companies determine the buying habits of Americans like you and me. All I'm saying is that what *you* think is just as important as the opinion of the next guy. If you find a subject you are passionate about, start doing some homework and research the statistics. See if others share your opinion, or if it is in complete contrast with the majority. Either way, there may be an opportunity to become a business consultant.

GETTING STARTED

Get your rear in gear and get started! Start *now* by looking around you. What do you see that needs to be improved? Remember, Visa, MasterCard, and American Express are where they are today because of Diner's Club. You don't hear much about Diner's Club anymore, do you? That's my point. Ticketmaster succeeded when Ticketron failed.

Looking to the computer world, remember how big and expensive those monstrosities were when they first came out? Now you can purchase lightweight laptops with all the power you need at a fraction of the price they once were. Remember the Model T by Ford? Contrast that today with a Mercedes sports coupe. The point is that many successful companies exist today because technology grew, or some smart entrepreneur saw the potential in an idea that was either poorly executed to begin with or one that didn't grow with the times.

Can you find a problem and solve it in such a way that the public will want to pay you a fee to make it better, whether it be a service or a product? Can you streamline a system or make something more user-friendly? The success of the For Dummies books is a result of the fact that they simplify numerous subjects from computers to spirituality, explaining them in terms that can be understood by even a "dummy." Readers are not embarrassed to be labeled as such. Rather, they flock to the bookstore shelves for available subjects because these books make things *easy*.

START SMALL

The creators of Subway, who I mentioned previously, started with one small shop and a modest budget of $1,000. Look where they are today. They are truly an American success story. They make sandwiches to order, and the customers know their sandwiches will be the same, no matter which location they visit.

But what if your entrepreneurial dream does not include having multiple locations? Success in *my* field, the mortgage industry, is often measured by the number of locations you have. After all, the more locations you have, the more money you make, right? Not necessarily. You will still have a significant overhead each time you add a new location. You want to make sure this new location will be cost-effective and, in fact, make a profit.

Banks and savings and loan associations would have a branch on every corner if it were feasible and cost-effective, thus making *convenience* their watchword. About 25 years ago, I worked in the marketing department of a savings and loan. The market research we conducted indicated that customers would accept lower interest rates on their savings accounts if the bank location were convenient, that is, near where they live or work. This was well before the Information Age and the Internet. Things have changed today, with online banking and access to investment opportunities across the globe, but this illustrates the fact that customers will sacrifice certain luxuries to make their lives easier in the long run.

Now, personally, I never had any desire to possess more than one location for my mortgage company. Sure, I've toyed with the idea, and I can't swear to you it will never happen, but I enjoy the personal interaction with my clients. It allows me to get to know them on a deeper level. I feel that the more I stray from my original concept, the further removed I become from personally helping people finance their homes, which is precisely what I enjoy doing.

I've also never had the need to see my company's name splashed all over town. It's not a good thing or a bad thing; it's just the way I feel.

What about you? What is *your* vision? Now I might suggest, at least initially, that you put aside your desire for grandeur and begin at a pace which is affordable and manageable. This is especially important if you are still currently employed and have responsibilities that prohibit you from embarking on a new full-time venture. An ideal enterprise for you would be to take a hobby or interest you have and build it into a viable business that ultimately translates into an opportunity to call your own shots.

My brother-in-law Charlie started his first company that way. He has a degree in accounting and was hired by a big firm upon graduating from college. He always enjoyed backpacking and camping, and eventually turned his love of the outdoors into an international business. He found that very few stores offered much when it came to freeze-dried foods suitable for camping trips. He began his business by offering a full menu of freeze-dried foods at low prices. He took out ads in small magazines, which eventually led to advertisements in large outdoor magazines. Ultimately, he was able to place his merchandise in major sporting-goods stores. Orders came from as far away as Japan. Not bad for a company that he started in a spare bedroom!

He had a plan. He decided what he wanted, slowly implemented his marketing, and then built a clientele that spanned the world. Charlie discovered he could do a better job for his clients than anyone else because he catered to their specific needs with the attention and care that they could not find anywhere else. He eventually quit his accounting job and has now developed and sold several businesses.

NAMING YOUR PERSONAL BUSINESS

One of the most important tasks of any business plan is choosing a name for that business. It should be something that is representative of your product or service. You want to make it as easy as possible for people to find you.

"The Mortgage Source, Inc.," informs people that my company operates within the mortgage industry. The name "Barnes and Noble Booksellers" says if you are looking for a book, then this is the place to go. You may have no idea who "Barnes" or "Noble" is, but that doesn't matter. The keyword is *Bookseller.* "Chem-Dry Carpet Cleaners" is self-explanatory, as is "ABC Stationery." If you can somehow incorporate a word or words describing what you do in the company name, it certainly can work to your advantage, especially if you are operating a new venture. When it comes to listings in the phone book, you have another advantage if you are at the beginning of the alphabet as opposed to the end. People pick up the Yellow Pages and go to the category in which they are interested. They almost always start in the beginning, calling the first few numbers until they get what they want. It's just human nature. That is something to consider if phone-book advertising is going to be a major source of business for you.

The names "Johnson Brothers," "Horace and Company," and "Monty and Associates" tell you absolutely nothing about the nature of the business. If someone is well-known either nationally, internationally, or even within their local market, a surname can effectively be used as the name of his or her company. Examples of this were given earlier in personality brands. If your name is not well-known, or is unknown to the public, ditch the ego and come up with a good name that tells everyone what you want to convey about your company.

Over the course of time, a company can be identified with the products it sells, e.g., "Proctor and Gamble" or "Johnson and Johnson." But creating an image and identification takes time and money. In a start-up venture, be sure to do all you can to help your clients understand exactly what you do, how it is different than what others do, and what the easiest and quickest way to find you might be.

ARE YOU AN ENTREPRENEUR?

Is it in you? Interestingly, I have found in many dissatisfied 9-to-5ers a concern that they are not entrepreneurial. They are therefore unable to fathom the concept of creating a business. I personally was unable to comprehend such a notion until I was so miserable that I had no choice.

In some cases, entrepreneurs create vital new concepts, and in other cases, they create companies that allow them to perform their specialized professions as only they can. The latter was my personal preference, and now I get to do things my way. Many home-buyers have told me that they were turned away by a number of lenders after being informed that they simply didn't qualify. These individuals felt that I gave them hope and encouragement, so that even if they couldn't purchase a home today, by following a financial plan and budget, they could buy a home in the next six months to a year. That's a long way from hearing, "You'll never own a house." My business has provided me with a sense of pride and fulfillment that I could not experience any other way.

LEMONADE-STAND INGREDIENTS

1. What do you expect from yourself? (This is obviously a broad question, so pick one area and narrowly define it.)

2. What is most exciting to you: having a partner, purchasing a franchise, manufacturing, improving an existing idea, or bringing a product to market?

3. How do you know you'll be a successful entrepreneur?

CHAPTER 5
THE MASTER PLAN: THE BLUEPRINT FOR YOUR LEMONADE STAND

Innovation distinguishes between a leader and a follower.
–Steve Jobs

Now we're going to get down to brass tacks, the heart and soul of your business. No matter how sophisticated your business idea, or how simplistic, it is imperative that you create a business plan and establish a budget for your company. It doesn't matter if you want to be a personal shopper or build computer security systems, you must know how much capital you'll need to establish your lemonade stand and whether it will be open full- or part-time. You will want to prepare a business budget as well as a personal budget. By that, I mean you need to determine how many units you will have to sell of whatever it is you provide in order to cover your business bills, leaving you with enough money to afford personal expenses such as food.

In my experience, I had to figure how much income I needed to generate to cover office expenses, utilities, insurance, supplies, postage, and salaries. Then I determined the number of loans I needed to close on a monthly basis, based on an average loan size and average commission. That allowed me to go back and review how many loans I was already closing per month when I was working for my former employer, my average loan amount, and what amount of income was being generated. By so doing, I was able to walk into my own business with some degree of comfort about what my game plan would be.

In the event you don't have former business data to rely on, then you will have to make projections based on information you do have. That might come from industry standards, interviewing others in the same business, reading the papers, looking for statistics online, or reviewing information provided by associations.

Now, whatever projection you came up with, use only 75% of it. It is better to be conservative in this instance and not overestimate your income. Things are going to come up unexpectedly, and you will find that income will ebb and flow. You can be sure that you will experience some fluctuations in the business cycle and in the marketplace. It's not unusual for companies to experience stronger sales during certain months than others.

If you are purchasing a franchise or an existing enterprise, then you will have to rely on facts and data provided to you by the corporate office to determine if this is a viable business for you. As a reminder from the previous chapter, ask for references and to speak with other franchise owners. Don't be afraid to interview them and ask if their expectations have been met or surpassed. Have they made the income that was expected in a given time frame? If not, how far away did they come? Has the corporate office lived up to their promises? What difficulties and frustrations have been experienced? What changes would they make if they could? On the other hand, what has gone better than expected? Has the corporate office been a dream to work with? Did they deliver what they promised? How has cash flow been so far? Are they finding that their companies are busier at certain times of the year than others?

It's always better to prepare for any and all circumstances when running a company. I am not a fan of seeing people put themselves in excessive debt, but as the owner of a business, you will find that there will be times when you require cash flow. I firmly believe that the best time to secure funds is *before* you need them. For example, if you are a homeowner, can you get an equity line of credit? This is a revolving line of credit that is reusable as you write checks and then pay off your balance. You are only charged interest when you write a check and have an outstanding balance. In today's competitive banking environment, many equity lines are available to obtain for little or no cost.

Having a line of credit may prove to be of great value to you during quiet business cycles. You see, your creditors don't necessarily care about how sales are going this month. All they care about is whether you are able to pay back the money you owe them or not. You can't exactly send a note to your creditors, as opposed to a check, indicating that sales are slower than you would like and that you will pay when you can. No, this is not advised.

If you are not fortunate enough to own a home, find out if your bank offers an unsecured line of credit. Basically, this means the loan is secured by your signature and your "good looks," as well as your good credit history and payment habits. If possible, plan your new venture in whatever spare time you have while still employed. This way, there is no pressure to make instant profits, and it will be easier to get credit while you are still drawing a paycheck.

Sometimes, however, you don't have that luxury. If you are unexpectedly let go from your employer, then you can't spend too much time brooding over it. Or, if you are like I once was and absolutely hate where you work, you may have to jump ship before you have your life preserver in place. I knew I wouldn't have lasted much longer at the company I worked for, so I started a little sooner than I would have liked.

At the time I opened my company, I made the mistake of calling vendors and telling them I wanted to go into business for myself. Even though I had been a commissioned salesperson in the same industry for years, and in essence, self-employed, no one wanted to extend credit to me. Maybe I was naïve, but this really surprised me. Luckily, I had a line of credit from years earlier, which I had never used. Well, let me tell you, I used it then. If you have the means to pay with cash or need very little money to start your company, then you are very fortunate, because there is no better feeling as a business owner than being debt-free.

After being open only a few short months, I received a call from American Express offering me a corporate credit card. I told them I wouldn't qualify for it, as my business had been operational for only a short time, and I had no financials to show them. They said it didn't matter. I didn't believe them and turned down their offer.

A few months later I received another call from American Express. Once more, I informed them of my new-business situation and that I could offer no documentation. Again, they said it didn't matter. "OK," I thought, "I'll call their bluff." I then accepted their offer, thinking there was no way it would happen. To my surprise, I received my corporate card in the mail within a few short days. Since then, they have sent additional credit cards and credit lines, and have made equipment loans available to me. I use credit sparingly, but there have been times when I would have been in trouble without it. It might be worth your while to check with American Express, Visa, MasterCard, or your bank to see what types of business credit lines, business credit cards, financing, or equipment leasing they might offer.

DO YOU HAVE A BUSINESS PLAN?

That's a fair question, isn't it? If you are going out on your own, you should know what your company does, what you are offering, and what your plan entails. Don't be nervous; it's not like you need to attend The Wharton School of Business. The idea of a business plan is to serve as a road map for you, to detail how you are going to get from point A (opening your personal business) to point Z (retiring from your personal business). A business plan is a working model that details how your business will *work*. A business plan may be created to serve your personal purposes only, or it can be a detailed analysis to raise capital from investors or bankers.

You need to determine what kind of venture you are going to open. Are you creating or inventing a product, or are you an independent contractor like a Realtor? Realtors, for example, are considered independent contractors even though they work for a specific company. A Realtor can post his license with a real-estate company of his choice, but is really responsible for creating and developing his own business.

Realtors need to be savvy business people because they generate their own listings, as well as their own buyers. They do get some help, as there is floor time where a designated Realtor receives and handles all sales calls. Calls may come from someone in their market who is interested in listing his home and, at the same time, inquires about purchasing a home. Realtors still need to treat real estate as if they are self-employed, because they only generate income when a transaction is consummated.

Another question to ask yourself is "How much capital will it take to establish yourself in your venture?" Are you working out of a spare bedroom or do you require office space? Must clients come to you or will you go to them? Or will you conduct all transactions over the phone or online?

The computer-repair technician, who has saved my backside on more than one occasion, doesn't need an office, as he regularly visits the offices of his clients. He needs a cell phone and a car, so he can go from place to place. He works out of his home when he needs to, but his clients don't visit him. Since my computer is in my office, he comes to me. He is definitely worth the price I pay, because besides possessing the experience and knowledge of the job at hand, he brings integrity to his profession.

Another important issue to consider is your budget for fixed costs, which are recurring monthly expenses and items you pay for whether you are generating income or not. This ties into whether you are going to have an office or work out of your home. If you are going to rent, then what is the monthly expense? How much money for the deposit and security fee is required at signing? What will it cost to purchase or lease a phone system? How much are business cards, stationery, envelopes, labels, file folders, paper, paper clips, and whatever else you might need? Should you have a Web site? How about furniture? Will you need a copier?

A note on phone systems: If you plan on having more than one incoming line, don't expect to walk into your local Radio Shack and pick up a phone that is ready to go. If you require more than one line, you will need a phone system that has multiple phone numbers, so when more than one call comes in at the same time, a busy signal will not be heard. Instead, simultaneous calls can be answered by a coworker or can roll over to voice mail. A simple phone system can easily add another $2,000 to your initial budget, and that is for a very simple system. The more sophisticated you get, as in the more lines you add and the more features your system has, the more expensive it becomes.

See, when you work for someone else, all that stuff is already there. It's been planned for and paid for. You never question how it got there, it just *is*. All you know is that one day, you showed up at the office, reported to work, and everything you needed was in place. Well, when it's *your* lemonade stand, *you* bring the lemons.

When I opened The Mortgage Source, Inc., I established a budget of $20,000. It was an amount I could afford, though I could have started up my business for less. At the same time, I knew others who spent four times as much.

Conversely, a friend of mine, Chuck Evans, opened Evans Financial Network in West Covina, CA, with $900. He used a spare bedroom in his house, had an extra phone line installed, ordered business cards and stationery, and was ready to go. Over the years, he built his company into a reputable business and now occupies a nice office space. What I admire about Chuck is that he didn't let anything stand in his way. He looked around at how other mortgage companies were operating and recognized an opportunity in his area to cater to clients, as he felt they deserved. Even though he started modestly, he was passionate about what he was doing and set a budget for what he could afford. He started slowly at the time, and has continued to expand his business over the past 20 years.

You may choose a lavish office with massive square footage in a prestigious building with marble floors. This would appear very impressive to prospective clients, but when you go down that avenue, it's important to remember that your fixed costs remain with you during all business cycles. I came from a large company with a fancy conference room, a super-deluxe photocopier, and a fully stocked kitchen. I quickly learned that starting out in my own venture, I could not afford such luxuries. Later, I realized that I never wanted the responsibility.

So now that we've talked about it, let's take a closer look at the ingredients that should go into a business plan. You will want to include and closely consider the following ingredients when writing your business plan:

1. **The name of your business.** What about the name do you like? Do you have alternatives in case the name is already taken? Ask reliable friends and family members for their opinions; they might have some valuable insight for you. Next, go online and do a search for the name you are considering. Do businesses similar to yours already exist with the same name? Besides causing confusion, you could also face some legal problems if you pursue that particular name. You could even be forced to change your company name if a competitor who established their business name and presence before you did pressures you to do so.

2. **The physical address and layout, even if inside your home, and the floor plan.** This might sound silly, but draw a diagram of your office space and where everything in it will be. This includes where the furniture will be (you want to make sure the furniture will fit within a given space), where people will sit, (even if it is just you), where the computer will be, where the fax machine or copier might rest, and where the phone will go. Take a look at where the electrical outlets and the phone jacks are. Are bathrooms nearby or a long distance away? Do you need a kitchen or water for your business? Consider *everything*, and take nothing for granted. Don't assume something can be brought in or added, because you may be wrong, or it could be very costly to do so.

3. **What your product or service will be and who your competition is, if any.** Really define your company or service. Get to know intimately what you are about to undertake and leave nothing to chance. If someone asked you to describe in just a few words the nature of your business, could you? Who is currently offering the same or similar prod-

uct or service? What makes what *you* are offering different or better?

4. If there is no competition, then how do you know there is a need for your business? If no one else is out there doing what you're doing, is there a good reason? Have you stumbled upon an idea that no one else has? Or have you come up with a business idea that no one needs or wants? For example, you may think about reintroducing the horse and buggy. Just because it's not currently being done, doesn't make it a good idea. It's difficult to create a need for your product if it doesn't already exist. The most successful products and services are born from problems that need to be solved.

5. Who is your primary target market? By that, I mean who will buy what you want to sell? Men? Women? Both? Is there a particular age group that might have more interest? These are your demographics. It is important to determine the answers to these questions because depending on who your target market is, demographics will dictate how you might communicate and market to prospective customers.

6. List all principals of the business and their work history, a résumé, per se, for each. If you are the only person working for the company, then this will be an easy task. You will want to do this no matter what, because if you are just starting out, people will want to know something about you. Also, if you are seeking investors, suppliers, financiers, or manufacturers, you will undoubtedly need to provide such information.

7. Annual financial projection for the first five years. It is better to be conservative, especially if you are seeking financial assistance. On what are your projections based? Industry averages? Information from a corporate office? Business trends? Or just a good guess? A good guess is the least desirable, as you are laying yourself on the line, investing your time as well as your money. Make sure you have reliable numbers to with which to formulate your financial projection.

8. The amount of capital you need to start up. Determine the capital for the purchase of all necessary equipment, computers, phones, office supplies, salaries, insurance, as well as a cushion for the unknown.

Start getting estimates for everything you will need. This is not a difficult task. You can shop online or peruse the phone book, but your
final figure should accurately reflect all of your initial purchases. Get
written estimates whenever possible.

A well-written and well-thought-out business plan can definitely help if
you are seeking venture capital. Venture capital is money you acquire from
others to put toward the creation of your business. Be sure to include passion in your plan: What separates you from others that will help you stand
out and be successful is the passion for what you want to do. Sometimes it
is the difference between getting the money you need or not, and being successful or not. I've heard many stories from bankers who said the decision
to loan money to someone ultimately came down to their love and passion
for their business.

Depending on the business climate, it can be difficult to find venture capital no matter how well-thought-out and written your plan. People, as well as
companies that specialize in start-up ventures, have the pick of the litter, so
they are going to obviously pass on most of what they see to cherry-pick exactly what they want.

This does not mean, however, that money is unavailable. You can look
for companies online and in the phone directory that specialize in equipment
leasing and commercial loans. You can search for money sources under the
categories *Investment Banking, Venture Capital, Minority Enterprise Small
Business,* or *Private Investors.* Many companies still get off the ground
because their founders have used available credit from their credit cards.

The Small Business Administration (SBA), was created in 1953 to coun-
sel, protect, and assist the interests of small businesses. It is an independent
agency of the federal government. According to the SBA Web site, small
business is vital to the U.S. economy because:

- Small-business firms account for over 99% of all employer firms
- Half of all employees are in the private sector

- More than 45% of the U.S. payroll is provided by small business

- Between 60% and 80% of all new jobs are created by small business

- 52% of all home businesses and 2% of franchises are small business

- Women own approximately 6.5 million businesses

- Minorities own over 4 million businesses

The SBA also offers information about training, hiring, and tax assistance, as well as the following:

- How to get a business loan

- How to get started in business

- How to get a business license

- How to get a Tax Identification Number

- How to get your business certified as woman-owned or minority-owned

The SBA provides billions of dollars of assistance annually. They have an extremely informative Web site; check them out at www.sba.gov.

You can also turn to relatives and friends for start-up money. You may not want to; it's a decision you have to make. Certainly don't put pressure on anyone, which can make him or her feel guilty or obligated. Do be sure to present potential investors with your business plan and properly represent the facts and potential risks. If someone wants to invest, give him the opportunity; he might feel that making an investment in *you* is a great investment! People make companies successful. As I said before, never underestimate the value that you bring to your business. Even though these are your friends and relatives—in fact, *especially* because they are—put everything you are offering in writing, so there are no misunderstandings later.

BUSINESS REALITY

Here's a sobering fact: As exhilarated as you might be as you embark upon your journey of entrepreneurship, the SBA reports that a staggering 95% of all businesses don't survive past five years. The primary reasons for this are poor planning and under-capitalization. Additionally, companies may very well fail if their owners are not truly following their heart's passion, but are just looking for a way to make money. Remember that owning a business will present challenges, and if you don't truly *love* what you do, more room for failure exists.

The real estate and mortgage industries are facing a change as I write this. Hopefully, the sub-prime meltdown will soon be a thing of the past. In the meantime, many companies have been forced into bankruptcy, have let go thousands of workers, or have just plain shut down. If you don't truly love what you do, don't have a passion for this industry, and are not willing to work harder than you ever have, then you will not survive. You have to have the problem-solving drive to stay alive.

SCORE ONE FOR THE LITTLE GUY

SCORE (Service Corps of Retired Executives) is a nonprofit organization with the sole purpose of assisting small-businesses with information, growth, and planning. Known as "Counselors to America's Small Business," they have 389 chapters in the United States and assist hundreds of thousands of entrepreneurs each year. SCORE is headquartered in Herndon, VA, and Washington, D.C., and was formed in 1964. You can schedule a face-to-face counseling session with their members or ask them questions via e-mail. They offer inexpensive workshops and offer a number of resources (www.score.org). SCORE offers free business advice and can help you build your business by fine-tuning your business plan, assisting you with a marketing plan, helping you to determine your budget, and suggesting ways to increase your cash flow.

Here are some of the topics they cover on their Web page:

1. Starting your business

2. Growing your business

3. Managing your business

4. Technology for your business

5. Financing your business

6. Tips on finding venture capitalists and investors

7. Information on state and local funding

8. Tips for marketing your Web site

9. Top five business tips

They also have a page that lists companies with which they have formed alliances that can assist small businesses. These companies include American Express, AOL for Small Business, American Management Association, Bank of America, Business Loan Express, and FedEx, to name but a few. SCORE is a resource partner of the Small Business Administration (SBA).

ACCOUNTING

As a personal business, you probably won't require the services of an accountant on a day-to-day basis. Still, it would be a good idea to interview a CPA or accountant who you can call on when needed. You can have your accountant handle your books for you, you can hire a bookkeeper, or you can do it yourself. There are a number of computer programs readily available at Staples or Office Depot that are easy to understand. I have an accountant who prepares my business returns for me during the year based on information I provide him. I really don't want to spend the time doing the accounting myself, so I would rather hire that out.

Before opening my company though, I met with my accountant a few times, I even brought my wife along for one meeting so that she could be involved and know what to expect. He helped me take a realistic look at what I was attempting to do, and that helped me to remain calm and stay focused. Normally, I only call him when needed, and send him tax information annually.

LEGALIZE

I firmly believe that the more you know, the better prepared you are to compete as an entrepreneur in the business world. I conferred with an attorney a number of times prior to opening my company to discuss business leases, how my company should be formed (see next section), hiring, contracts, and liability. I know others who flew by the seat of their pants and took the attitude that they would seek answers only when questions arose. Personally, I don't want to run a company that way; I like being prepared. It's a matter of your comfort level. With the Internet, it seems you can find many things you need. There are also several books published by Nolo Press about doing your own legal work. You may also consult with a paralegal. While not attorneys, paralegals are well-adapted to the legal processes. Some people just don't want to pay for legal services; though I suggest, if possible, that you consider it. It could be the best money you ever spend.

METHODS OF OPERATING A BUSINESS

You will have to decide how your company should be formed and how it will operate. By that, I mean there are different formats for a business, and you will want to choose what works best for you. For example, I have mentioned partnerships in a previous section, and we will take a more in-depth look at them in this chapter, but you can also operate your business as a sole proprietor, a corporation, or a Limited Liability Company (LLC).

A sole proprietorship is probably the easiest and least-expensive way to open your lemonade stand. You might need to obtain a business license, depending on the rules of your local government, or pay some other types of fees. Basically, you file your business name, open your doors, and you are ready to go.

You'll need to file a *fictitious business statement* with a newspaper of general circulation, that is, a local newspaper. It does not have to be a major publication such as the *Los Angeles Times, The New York Times,* or the *Chicago Tribune.* Usually there are salespeople outside the City Recorder's office or courthouse waiting to take your information. They make it as easy as possible to publish your business name, and the cost runs under $20. When it comes time to open a bank account, you will take a copy of this filing as proof to your business bank of choice and open a bank account. You may have to show them a business license, if applicable.

As a sole proprietor, you have no name protection. This means that it is very possible to have more than one company with the same name, even in your same area of service. You may be forced to change your business name if someone in a similar business is operating under the same name in your same area. For name protection, you need to consult with a business attorney or an intellectual-property attorney. As a sole proprietor, you and your business are one. That means if someone seeks damages against your company, you are personally responsible for any liability, should a judgment be obtained.

A **partnership** exists when you have more than one principal in a company. You are not required to form a partnership agreement, though it may be advised. Partners are responsible for the actions of other partners. As a result, you should consider having an attorney draw up a partnership agreement stating exactly who does what and who is responsible for what. It should include an exit clause, should one or more partners choose to leave the business before the others. It's not always the case that everyone gets along within a partnership. However, these entities exist for the mutual benefit of all concerned.

A **corporation** is recognized as a legal entity and is the most complex of all business structures. Stock ownership dictates who has a controlling interest and say-so in the company. There are do-it-yourself kits to incorporate yourself, if you feel inclined to do it this way. A corporation can exist even if there is only one person in the company. That person then owns 100% of the stock. Don't let this confuse you. Oftentimes we think of stock as something only bought and sold on the New York Stock Exchange. The public can buy stock in companies listed on the Exchange because they are publicly owned companies. This means that as a private citizen, you can purchase shares of a company that you believe to be a good investment. Most corporations are private, like mine. Yes, I own all the shares, but since it is not being traded, it only means something to me.

A corporation can enter into legal agreements, buy and sell property, sue, and be sued in a court of law. As the owner of a small corporation, you may, however, be required to personally guarantee any financial dealings into which you enter. Don't be surprised if this is indeed a requirement. Liability is limited to the assets of the corporation.

If you incorporate, you will need a Tax Identification Number, also known as a "95 Number." In the case of a sole proprietorship, you report your income as part of your personal tax return, filed under your Social Security number. As a corporation, you file a separate return with a Tax Identification Number. You can obtain a Tax ID number by contacting the Internal Revenue Service and requesting Form SS4. This form is also available on the IRS's Web site: http://www.irs.gov.

As I mentioned, you don't have to be a large publicly owned company to be a corporation. My company was incorporated for two reasons: One was to make the company sound more established than, say, "XYZ Mortgage." The second reason was for legal protection.

A **Limited Liability Company (LLC)** is a bit different from both a corporation and a partnership in that it allows for the advantage of limited liability as a corporation and for pass-through taxation, as a partnership has. This means that income is reported as part of the members' personal tax returns on their Schedule C, or Profit and Loss Statement of the tax return. An LLC could still pay a substantial tax, based on gross receipts.

A corporation is taxed on either a calendar year or a fiscal year. A calendar year runs from January through December. In my case, I incorporated in June, so my fiscal year runs from June 1 through May 31. As a small corporation, it is easy for me to zero out my account and pay a minimum corporate tax of $800 per year. If the corporate account is not emptied, I pay a tax on the amount of unspent capital, thus the term *double taxation.*

As with any of the above ways of forming a business, you can do it yourself if you choose to do so. Then again, you can also perform surgery on yourself if you so desire. I think it's a better idea to call a doctor.

BANKING

One of the best parts of my job is going to the bank and making deposits into my account. However, in order to do this, you need a business account. Choose a bank that is business-friendly and that offers services to personal businesses, such as business credit cards, leasing, and loans. They may even assist you in accepting credit-card payments from your clients and offering a payroll service. If you are incorporated, you will need to bring your Articles of Incorporation as well as your 95 Number to the bank. If you are a sole proprietor or a partnership, they will either want to see a copy of your partnership agreement or other proof that you are, in fact, a legal business.

BUSINESS INSURANCE

Business insurance protects the contents of your office from loss due to fire and theft. Even if you work out of your home, it is something you should consider. If you lease or rent office space, your landlord will most likely require it, as well as liability insurance, in case anyone is injured on your premises. There is also insurance for business interruption. For example, if your office is destroyed by fire or another catastrophe, you are still insured and actually receive income even though your office is shut down.

If you are selling or have created a product, then you will want to have (or in some instances, will be *required* to have) product insurance. This is in case someone is injured by or harmed by your product. In the case of our 13-hour clock, we were required to carry product insurance before we could sell it to a catalog company. The catalog wanted to make sure that if some harm befell the purchaser of our clock, they would not be liable.

If you have coworkers, you may be required to have worker's compensation insurance, in case anyone is injured on the job. This pays employees while they are out and protects your company's funds.

If you are your family's principal wage-earner, or the *only* wage-earner for that matter, you may also want to consider disability insurance, should anything happen to you. If you become injured and unable to work, you will still collect an income. Consider also life insurance to protect your family in the event you die. As is the case with having a good accountant and attorney, a trusted insurance agent is a valuable asset.

PURCHASING COMPUTERS AND OTHER OFFICE EQUIPMENT

I first seriously considered opening my own company in April 1992, and in the two months that followed, I did my homework—my due diligence. Since this was before existence of the Internet, I was limited to the phone book, newspaper classified ads, and people who knew people. If you spend the time, you can ferret out great deals. Remember, you don't need to buy everything *new*. Instead, you can buy used items or even consider leasing.

Ask your friends—actually anyone you know—what they know about the equipment you are seeking. You never know when someone might be aware of some great deal that you are not. When it came time to purchase office furniture, one friend of mine told me about a business-furniture clearance sale where I was able to purchase six desk-and-chair sets, file cabinets, and bookshelves—all for $300!! Now you couldn't furnish a palace with it, but it did the trick for my small business.

My next purchase on the list was a photocopier. Have you priced those things? I mean, a really nice one! This was a difficult task for me because in the mortgage business, it's very easy to make thousands of copies each month. I needed something durable, reliable, with an automatic feeder and sorter. One problem: price. A new copier alone can sell for upwards of $7,500. I had no doubt that was way outside of my budget. As chance would have it, I found an ad in the paper for used copiers and purchased one with all the features I needed for only $1,500. I was able to purchase a service agreement so that if anything went wrong, I was covered. That copier lasted six years. I spent more in service warranties over the years than for the copier itself, but that was not a problem. In my line of work, if your copier is down, then so are you.

The most expensive office item I required was a computer. The investment for a brand-new IBM-compatible 486 computer (that was the hot model back then) fully loaded with printer and monitor was $3,000. That was 15 years ago. In the years that followed, prices dropped dramatically and I have purchased two of these for much less.

I spent $2,400 on my office lease, including first and last months' rent, furniture for $300, $1,600 for a phone system, $900 to the phone company for new phone lines, $500 for business insurance, $200 for a typewriter (we still needed typewriters back then), $250 for a fax machine, and $250 for stationery supplies. The rest went into my business account to cover expenses for the first few months, because I figured I might need 60 to 90 days to begin generating income. I was lucky in that I closed my first loan about 30 days after I opened my company.

At the end of the first week of opening my company, I still remember the feelings I experienced. I was exhilarated and excited, and I gazed around my office, amazed by what I had accomplished. It was Friday night, the office was closed, and I didn't want to leave. I had done more than I'd ever believed possible. I had my own company, my own personal business, my own lemonade stand. I was officially open! I couldn't have been prouder.

LEMONADE-STAND INGREDIENTS

1. Determine the business, industry, or service you plan to enter.

2. Complete your business plan.

3. Establish your budget.

4. Determine how much capital you will need to start your venture.

5. Determine where the money will come from. Do you have investors, partners, a bank loan, an equity line, or credit cards?

CHAPTER 6
THE KINDNESS OF STRANGERS: MARKETING YOUR LEMONADE STAND

In marketing I've seen only one strategy that can't miss—and that is to market to your best customers first, your best prospects second, and the rest of the world last.
　　— **John Romero**

You've planned your work and you've worked your plan; you've probably heard this a million times. In other words, you are about ready for business. Now what? Well, if no one knows you exist, it doesn't matter how good a job you can do for people! So, what should you do? The first thing many people think of is advertising on television, on the radio, or in print. It's easy to consider advertising as a means of getting your business name out there. Paid spots are available on radio, television, or in print, where you control where your message will be seen and at approximately what time. What you can't necessarily control is who will see your spot and if it will be effective. You won't know these things until after it runs and you receive the results.

In theory, if you purchase ad time on radio or television, or in print media, you can choose the program, magazine, or newspaper that speaks to your demographic. As a result, you will have a pretty good idea of who's watching, listening, or reading. You can also target a particular socioeconomic group within a certain age range and gender. You can purchase this airtime or print ad, but through no fault of your own, you may fail to reach the people you want.

Let's say you advertise luxury cars during a sporting event, and a school kid is watching that program right when your commercial appears. It may be impossible for the kid to purchase your product even if he wanted to because it's not affordable for him. Now perhaps someday it will happen; maybe you are building a customer in waiting, still hibernating, as it were, but that doesn't help you now. You are depending on the program in which you purchase advertising to draw the particular demographic you are seeking.

Besides, advertising can be expensive. You have to consider not only the cost of the ad time, but also the cost of production, including cast, crew, camera, lighting, etc. Then you pay a fee every time your ad runs. You can't run a commercial once and think you are done advertising your business. It's the *frequency* that matters. This means it may take several repetitions of your commercial on many stations before your message registers with a potential customer. It could take a combination of everything—television, radio, and print ads—to establish yourself with an audience. Unless you are well-capitalized or a national company with a large budget, the money you spend could be wasted, because it takes months, if not years, to make inroads with your desired clientele, especially if you are a new establishment.

A side note here: Many cities have their own local newspapers, magazines, or even cable advertising opportunities. It can be a good idea to see what is being done in your area and to investigate the cost of running an ad in a local paper or magazine. Residents of an area often read these resources, specifically with the intent of calling someone local who has placed an ad. In addition, small papers and magazines need content. See if you can provide a story about you, your company, or your involvement in the community that would be newsworthy. A few ideas include hosting a seminar, sponsoring a local event, and becoming involved in city government.

My firm, The Mortgage Source, Inc., is a small company. There is no way I can compete with the advertising money the larger companies spend, let alone the multibillion dollars that banks and savings institutions spend. No way! So I have to compete in a different way.

BE CREATIVE

I have to let people know that they are working with the president and owner of the company, one who has over 29 years of experience. *They will receive my personal attention and expertise.* If they call a bank or savings and loan, they don't know with whom they are going to speak. For example, if they call a bank, they are not going to talk to the owner of the bank, the CEO, or the president, but instead, a representative of the bank. That's what makes large companies large.

I have to compete, playing to *my* strengths, not to someone else's. If this were a sports competition, I would have to establish a strategy where I set my own pace, rather than reacting to the moves of my opponent.

A large bank might tell you how big they are and how long they've been around, but so what? The size and strength of a company has no bearing on you. If you are sold on borrowing money from a bank because they are big and think that they are sound, well, don't worry about them going out of business. If you borrow money from them, then *they* need to worry, not you. And if you have deposits, then they are federally insured against loss.

What consumers care about is **what companies can do for them**, not the other way around. Doing business with a large company only makes them larger, and thus serves their needs. If someone with whom you are considering doing business tells you his company is the biggest or has been around since before the beginning of time, and that is the only thing he has to tell you about his company, either ask him pointed questions or move on to someone else. Questions I would ask include:

1. How does the size of your company help me? If the answer is a self-serving one and doesn't address your specific needs, then keep looking.

2. How does the age of your company help me? Many salespeople associate the age of their company with name awareness, as if they are the standard in the industry. This may or may not be true. You still have to

come back to the question of how *your* needs are going to be served.

SPREADING THE WORD

So, how do you let people know about your company and your product or service? Well, there is no substitute for word-of-mouth advertising. That means that clients are singing your praises about what a great job you did in meeting their needs. They become a walking commercial to other targeted buyers who are seeking what you are selling. It is important to understand that this is a sure-fire way to reach exactly the people you want to inform about your product or service, and it comes with a personal recommendation. As already stated, if you purchase ad time on television or other media, you could be easily spending a small fortune but wasting money. You could be missing your target or reaching others who could care less about what you do, aren't in the market for it, already have it, or can't afford it.

The first thing I would do is send out written announcements to everyone in my network, letting them know that my company is open and I am ready to serve their needs. Include several business cards. Remember when, in a previous chapter, I mentioned the importance of networking? Well, now you can see how this will come into play. People are eager to give you a chance and will do all they can to work with you and your company.

Word-of-mouth advertising takes you to the core of your target market. Plus, you receive the endorsement of someone who knows you, who already has experience with your company, and who is more than satisfied with the results. Fantastic!

Now settle down a minute. As good as this sounds, it does take time to build that kind of marketing. We still have to deal with the challenge of creating an avenue for people to come to you in the first place.

David, the CPA I mentioned, told me he built his clientele over a period of time. He interned and acquired his needed hours while working with a major accounting firm. He then told everyone he knew that he was going out on his own. In the beginning, it was important to keep his overhead low so he wouldn't succumb to the pressure of having to build his clientele and make a living at the same time.

David went on to fulfill his dreams of creating his own lemonade stand on the corner. He said that when he was starting out, his house payment was $946 per month, and if he was lucky, he would net that much. But the more people he helped, the more referral business he received, and his bandwagon kept on growing. Now he has a thriving practice as well as other investments and properties.

My friend John is a phenomenal tailor. Oh, the things he can do with material, scissors, and thread! He works out of a spare bedroom in his apartment. That's right; he's not on a major street with lots of drive-by traffic. There's no large sign on his building or even a telephone listing in the Yellow Pages. Amazing as it sounds, it's not unusual to show up at his home and have to wait while other people either drop off clothing to be measured and tailored or pick up finished goods, even if you have an appointment. But no one minds the wait. We all tell John to take his time because we all know that John will take care of us better than anyone else will, and he won't let us leave until our clothes look like a million bucks! On top of that, his prices are very reasonable. But that's not the point; it's the job he does and how he takes care of us. I would gladly pay him more, and have offered to do so, but John refuses, only charging what he feels he should. If you bring a garment to him, and he feels he can't do something the way he thinks you would like it done, he will tell you.

I'll never forget the time my wife went to a department store's closeout sale. There were bargains galore, but the garments were in limited sizes. She found a beautiful suit that was, without exaggeration, four sizes too large. "Perfect," she said after trying it on. And it was—after John finished recutting it. He spent half an hour alone just measuring the pleated skirt to make sure it would fit correctly. Once John was finished altering it, the suit looked custom-made. The fact that the price he charged for his service was a fraction of what we thought it should be made the whole experience that much more unbelievable. As I said, we would have gladly paid more. My wife wanted it to look perfect; and it did! Recently, John revealed his secret to me.

"Victor," he said, "I have over 250 steady customers who come to me on a regular basis. Do you know how it all started?"

I had never really thought about it.

"No," I replied.

"With you and one other client. That's how it all began. The two of you began spreading the word about me, and then [those you told] told others who told others, and it is because of that, I am where I am today."

I corrected him. "It's because of the way you take care of your customers that you are where you are today."

He smiled.

You can't have one without the other. If you do a great job but nobody knows, you're in trouble. And if people know about you, but you do a lousy job, you're in trouble.

John wants all of his clients to be as happy as possible. He never proves them wrong. By that, I mean, if a client asks him to do something, and he does it, but they are not happy, he never says, "But that's what you said you wanted." Instead, he makes changes or corrections until the client is pleased with the finish product. His lemonade stand has a line around the block consisting of people who want what he has. You can't do better than that.

If I hadn't been a satisfied customer, I would never have told anyone else about him. I've been a customer of his since 1973, and still am to this day. He has never advertised on radio or television, nor has he placed an ad in the paper. He doesn't have an office or a big sign where he works. Instead, he works out of his home, which offers him the ability to offer low prices and work with clients on a one-on-one basis.

15 YEARS IN BUSINESS

I just recently celebrated 15 years in business, which prompted me to examine my own experience with word-of-mouth advertising. I realize how my own production has grown on an annual basis since I opened my company in 1992. This is all due to the referral process and people spreading the word about me. Word-of-mouth advertising is like compound interest; it grows on a daily basis. Your clients' satisfaction is at the root of it. People love to brag to others when they get a great deal, receive superb service, or are treated in an extraordinary way. We all appreciate such treatment.

LOW-COST ADVERTISING IDEAS

There are a number of things you can do which are classified as advertising that really don't cost much and help to get your company name out to the public.

1. We don't often think about it, but something as simple as a business card is a form of advertising. Resist the temptation to create a card for very little or no money. In many cases, the first thing someone sees of your company is your business card. You may even consider using both sides of the card to set you apart.

2. Design a nice brochure for your company. You can make them yourself on a computer if you feel you can do a sufficient job. Be sure to detail your company or service, as well as yourself. Brochures do a fine job of selling for you.

3. If you are serving a small community or a specific industry, consider printing flyers that detail your business. For example, I can make flyers that spell out interest rates or programs in lending, and then place them in Realtors' mailboxes. If you are considering going door-to-door through your target neighborhood, there are some restrictions on placing items without a stamp in mailboxes. Check out the rules in your area so that you won't have any problems.

4. Discount certificates are also a nice way of introducing the public to your company, and it gets them in the door. Of course, you want to do a bang-up job of whatever it is that you do so that customers will return. The whole point of a discount certificate is to give people a reason to come to you in the first place. In this case, the reason is to save money.

So don't skimp on these clients. Instead, go overboard for them, so they will come back and tell others about you as well.

Make sure your advertising looks professional, is attractive, and communicates the message you are trying to send. Ensure that the material you produce is easy to read and that it includes information like your company name, business address, phone number, Web site, and e-mail. You are trying to make it as easy as possible for people to do business with you.

THE ROLE OF PUBLIC RELATIONS

Rob Deigh, owner of RDC Communication/PR, (rdeigh1@aol.com) says that public relations is a vital tool to entrepreneurs if used effectively. "It's another way to get your name out into the public, and it doesn't have to cost a lot."

Rob defines public relations as "the art of communication for all of your important messages." He notes, "You want people to take notice of what you can do for them and help them make the right decision."

Rob suggests that you:

1. Become clear about what you want to convey in your message to the public. He suggests nailing three or four important topics to which a customer or potential customer will respond.

2. Make sure your message is consistent and is included in all your correspondence, as well as present on your Web site and in your presentations.

3. Meet press people in your area if possible. What are the stories of the people inside your organization aside from the work they do? For example, do they paint pictures, sing, dance, or write novels? Is there someone who the press might want to interview? The press is looking for stories of interest, not for ways to promote your company. A story can be conveyed through the owner of the company, the president, or

even a customer who has had experience with your company. Do a study or a survey and write about the results.

Spend time at least once a week, if not more often, working on material to promote yourself and your business. You can communicate with the public through your blog, your Web site, and all personal correspondence. Rob also suggests you write articles for your local business journal and industry papers. Write about topics that are interesting, provide some practical tips for the public, and become the go-to guy (or gal) when the press needs information. Find out what your local press wants, and introduce yourself to a few reporters if possible.

Willy Spizman, CEO of The Spizman Agency (www.spizmangency.com), a public-relations firm in Atlanta, GA, believes that older entrepreneurs "intrinsically understand the importance of how their business may be viewed in the marketplace." He notes that they ask themselves questions, for example: "Do we have a good reputation? Does our product or service live up to or exceed our customers' expectations?"

"Public relations helps build that reputation, and begins to brand the product or service in the mind of the consumer," notes Willy. He goes on to explain that your ultimate goal with public relations is to establish your brand and therefore, create a bond with your target audience. "This is accomplished through strategies that are based on creating emotion-filled relationships between the product or service and the consumer."

Willy recommends that public relations be a part of your daily business plan, no matter what business you are in. To illustrate his point, he notes that while some people consider accounting a boring industry, accountants are quoted in the media daily and as a result, their companies receive huge benefits because they have positioned themselves as experts. "Editorial coverage is value you can't buy, and it carries infinitely more weight than advertising."

When budgeting for public relations, Willy says that a campaign can take several months to plan and therefore, you should budget for a monthly retainer. In general, they start at about $2,000 per month and increase from there.

Another alternative is to pay hourly if you are seeking a consultation only. "A successful ongoing PR campaign takes a huge time commitment dozens of hours to plan and implement, so retainers will give you the most bang for your buck."

PUBLIC SPEAKING

Another way to promote your company or business and yourself is by speaking publicly about what you have to offer. Now before you close the book, get up, and leave, hear me out. I know that many people dread the idea of speaking in public, and would prefer to undergo an IRS audit than stand up in front of a group of people. That is a little dramatic, isn't it? Think of the benefits of public speaking. You have a captive audience who is there to see *you* and listen to what *you* have to say. How much better can it get?

Nancy Tierney of Unconditional Confidence (www.unconditionalconfidence.com) "liberates entrepreneurs from their fear of public speaking," as she puts it, and "helps each person find his or her own charisma." She admits that speaking can be a bit harder for entrepreneurs over 50, especially if they don't have experience in the past, but Tierney wants people to move away from the belief that speaking is difficult and instead, find enjoyment in it. She notes that you can find plenty of opportunities to speak within your chosen market, through service groups, the chamber of commerce, the Rotary Club, the Lions Club, churches, and synagogues. Many local papers or journals publish weekly group gatherings and where they meet, and as a result, are always looking for speakers. When you do find a group to address, conduct a small investigation to ensure that your message is consistent with that which they are seeking.

Tierney also suggests that you give something away every time you speak to a group. It can be one of your products, someone else's product, or even a gift card from Starbucks. Collect business cards as an incentive and then give away a prize.

She offers the following tips to inexperienced speakers:

1. When you plan your talk, "go deep, not wide." By this, Tierney means, spend 10 minutes per topic so that you give your listeners quality information. Don't try to pack too much into a small period of time, because they won't remember it all. She feels that if you present only a few content-filled topics, your audience will respect you and equate you with value.

2. Concentrate on your content, not your style. We all want to be entertaining, funny, and polished in our presentation skills, but the message is king. Don't get hung up on not being good enough. "Just talk; you already know how to do that." You will improve as you speak on more occasions. Care more about your message and what you are offering than how you offer it. Have fun!

3. Don't worry about how to do it, and don't freak yourself out. Look for a friendly face in the audience. Speak to that one person, and then move on to the next. It's easier to do it this way than trying to connect to the entire audience as a whole.

4. Trust your nervous system, and know that you are going to be fine. Don't try to suppress the way you feel, because all you are doing is making your fear grow bigger and thus, creating more tension. Your nervousness will begin to diminish as you are ready.

Tierney acknowledges there is an initial fear when we start to speak due to adrenaline racing through our bodies. She is a former neuromuscular therapist and in her practice, learned how the nervous system works. "You feel your heart pounding and your body shake, which is the work of the *sympathetic nervous system*, in essence, fight or flight. This happens to everyone. But after a while we calm down due to the *parasympathetic nervous system*, which acts to balance us.

Tierney wants you to realize that when you notice these things happening in your body, there is nothing to worry about; it is just energy moving, so let it move. To help calm yourself, take a deep breath and don't feel like you have to launch into your opening. Greet everyone in attendance and thank him or her for inviting you. Then when you are ready, begin slowly and take your time throughout.

BLOGGING

A blog is a type of Web site that is informal in nature. It allows you to communicate your message on the Internet about events happening in your industry or, for that matter, really anything you wish. A company Web site, in contrast, is a very formal introduction to your company. It provides your guests with information about the company, its services, and its owners, and perhaps offers customers the opportunity the ability to purchase products online.

In a blog, you can offer your viewpoint on changes within your industry, current trends, and new innovations. A blog can even be part of your company Web site. Most blogs are updated on a regular basis, which can be weekly, daily, or even hourly. The important thing is to be consistent and add fresh content whenever possible to keep people interested in reading what you have to say. Many people use events in their lives to write about, so if you have a new company, then you will have lots of content. Besides writing about your business, you can write about new advances in your industry, experiences with clients, new products and services—anything that you want.

To promote your blog, publicize it in your newsletter, or add it to your Web site. Write articles for whomever you can, and say something like, "Read my blog daily at www.YOUR_URL_HERE.com for up-to-date information." You can also search online for E-zines (publications on the Web) that are looking for content to publish. This all drives traffic back to your blog, and hopefully, to your Web site.

You can purchase computer software to create a highly sophisticated blog, or you can utilize free services available on the Internet. Some free blog services are located at www.wordpress.com, www.blogger.com, and www.typepad.com. The free services might be a bit more limiting in terms of what you can do; however, you can still create your own look and feel, as you can choose from one of many predesigned templates, color combinations, and word styles. Not bad, when you consider that it's free.

WHAT IS MARKETING?

It can be difficult to define the difference between marketing and selling. Inherently, you might know the difference. The two are closely related and yet completely different; selling is part of the marketing process.

I remember that the difference finally became crystal clear to me several years ago when I was district manager for a savings and loan association. I was interviewing a prospective loan representative who was eager and energetic, yet who lacked the real experience I was seeking. I knew that hiring him would mean a commitment of time, patience, and energy. It came down to one question in the interview that would make it or break it for him. I asked him what the difference is between selling and marketing.

He didn't hesitate when he answered. "**Selling is a one-time experience.** Maybe it's done over the phone or behind the counter. But once the sale is made and completed, that ends the relationship. **Marketing is the ongoing cultivation of a relationship** to satisfy the clients' needs on an ongoing basis."

Throughout the remainder of the interview, we discussed the different methods of marketing. But his was one of the best and most succinct definitions I have ever heard. Perhaps there exists a better selection of words or superior grouping of phrases, but this defined exactly what I needed to know about him, and reminds me of how I want to conduct my own business dealings. Some further distinctions will be made later concerning selling and marketing, though this explanation suffices for now. And by the way, I did hire the young man.

The point to remember about marketing is that you want to create a constant and consistent plan. You will be better served if you know how you want to go about this before you open your lemonade stand. Marketing is an important part of your business plan—one that requires you to budget for an ongoing expense. Sending out announcements is marketing. Distributing your business cards is marketing. Writing your letter on company stationery is marketing. These are just some of the basics.

It's very easy to ignore a marketing plan and put it on the back burner. Once you start making money, you should establish a marketing campaign.

One of the hardest things to do is to spend money when you are not making any. Not doing so is also one of the biggest mistakes people make in business today. The reason is that if you are not budgeting and planning your marketing today, there may not be a tomorrow. You can't assume clients will beat a path to your door just because you have an "OPEN" sign.

Your marketing efforts don't have to cost a fortune either. Investigate what would best represent you and your company within your particular industry. Now by this, I don't mean it has to be boring or stale. Be creative, if you can, and think outside the box. Use humor if it is appropriate. Sometimes being outrageous makes an impression with a particular clientele. Be sure to be professional and use good judgment, no matter what.

With advancements in technology, you can design, create and print marketing materials yourself. These same projects would have been just a dream only a few short years ago. The bottom line is that you don't need to spend your last dollar to make a name for yourself, to stand apart from others, or to get your name out to your target market. In the next chapter, I will discuss the significance of branding and how it applies to your company. Then we will examine many inexpensive suggestions to put your personal business on the map and have a great time in the process. Branding is a large part of marketing, and the two go hand in hand.

LEMONADE-STAND INGREDIENTS

1. What immediate opportunities do you recognize in front of you to promote your new venture?

2. What do you feel makes you unique?

3. What can you or your company do that no one else can for the client?

4. Do you have a clear message that represents what you do?

5. What low-cost advertising or marketing ideas do you have?

CHAPTER 7
BRANDING YOUR PERSONAL BUSINESS: THE BEST LEMONADE ON THE BLOCK

A brand is a living entity—and it is enriched or under-mined cumulatively over time, the product of a thousand small gestures.
— Michael Eisner

So much of what has been discussed and planned for from the beginning of this book to now leads to one thing: *branding*. Branding is a concept that has been applied intentionally or unintentionally in business for years and, in essence, creates a lasting impression in the consumer's mind to distinguish your service or product and require it, as opposed to that of your competition.

You may think you understand branding, but it's really difficult to get a grasp of such a concept. This is because it can mean different things to different people. Some people with whom I spoke said that branding pertains only to the name of one's company or product. Others said it had to do with one's logo and slogan. In reality, it has to do with all of these and more.

When I first heard the word *branding*, I immediately thought of the branding of cattle on the open range back in the days of the Old West. Ranchers branded a permanent impression on all of the animals within each herd. In much the same way, a business owner wants to leave an indelible impression or mark on the public.

If it were only as easy to do as it is to say, we would all be experts. Branding is successful when the public associates a generic item with your product name. For example, if someone asks for a Kleenex, as opposed to a tissue, that is an example of branding. We don't photocopy something; we Xerox it. When we go computer shopping, we are either seeking a PC or a Mac.

If we want to get a hamburger, what goes through our mind? Do we want a Double-Double, a Whopper, or a Quarter Pounder? While these are product names and none of them are synonymous with hamburger, each company would like you to think so. The companies that sell these products use branding to evoke emotions in us, causing the consumer to request their specific products. In-N-Out Burger says their hamburger is made the old-fashioned way, while Burger King says they will make your burger "your way," and McDonald's claims you'll love their offerings. Each wants you to smack your lips and request its own particular product. Each wants that for different reasons, though the end result is the same: revenue.

Companies are trying to satisfy not only our appetites, but also our emotions. Let's face it; we can consume any number of foods, but manufacturers want us to request only their specific products, which they claim will satisfy our senses as well as our appetites. We are a society that often eats even though we are not hungry. Food companies have successfully convinced us that consuming their products will fill the gaping holes in our lives. Branding is as much about satisfying our emotions as it is about fulfilling our needs.

We've been conditioned as consumers to purchase our *wants*, not our *needs*. For example, we need transportation, but do we need "no boundaries" like the Ford Explorer promises us? We need to get to work, but does it have to be in "The Ultimate Driving Machine"? You get the idea. Truthfully, any functioning automobile can get you to work or wherever you want to go. But we are conditioned to want *more* than just a plain automobile. We want it to be sporty, fast, luxurious, and/or showy—at least that's how automobile manufacturers want us to think.

Branding is establishing an identity separate from anyone else's, even though similar products may exist. A good brand becomes the core of the business. Branding is not just a slogan or catchy phrase; it is something that creates images and emotions in the minds and hearts of the public at large.

For many years, Levi Strauss & Co.'s ads told the story of how long their jeans had been in existence and how sturdy they felt when wearers descended into the mines to pan for gold. That image has evolved as Levi added more styles as well as products to their line. Now their focus is more on lifestyle and how their fashions add to it. Since most modern-day people no longer mine for gold, the need to focus on something else—in this case, lifestyle—was born.

Household Finance told you to "never borrow money needlessly, but when you must, call Household Finance." They were known simply by their initials: HFC. I must have been somewhat influenced by their brand because I actually worked for them back in the late 1970s.

When cigarette ads were allowed on television, companies weren't just selling smoking, but, rather, a complete image. These companies wanted to take you to "Marlboro Country" where you could be in the great outdoors, rounding up cattle. (I can't think of the last time I was out in the wilderness rounding up cattle.) Or, they wanted you to "be cool" by smoking only Kool cigarettes. Benson and Hedges built a reputation on being "just a silly millimeter longer." They didn't tell you how good they tasted, or that they were better, but only that you got more for your money. That's how they built their brand: by being fractionally longer than their competition. These ads were around when I was a kid, and yet I still remember them!

Successful branding distinguishes you from all others and enhances your perceived value, whether you offer a service or a product. It will assist you during a slow economy, as well as inspire customers to seek you out during good times because you will be preferred to your competition. A successful brand adds to customer recognition, appreciation, loyalty, and trust.

When you purchase athletic equipment, is there a specific brand you prefer? Maybe the shoes make you faster, the clothes make you lighter, and the accessories make you more attractive. Or, perhaps you just feel they do. No matter what the reason, you are demonstrating brand loyalty.

Lack of successful branding is one reason for the failure of Internet companies during the dot-com boom. With so many companies vying for your attention and so few established identities, it is understandable why many went belly-up.

You are the difference as far as the client is concerned. If you are recognized as a brand yourself, then the client wants you! This is the crux of it all, right here. If you understand this and realize that you are a unique brand, and you can impress this upon the public, then you have hit a crucial point of critical mass. Success is waiting for you on the other side.

Consider for a moment how many travel sites there are online—how many gift sites there are, automobile sites, mortgage sites. Do you type in a specific Web address when you seek information related to a particular subject, or do you just "Google" the general category? It can be difficult to distinguish one business from another, unless they have paid (or used/purchased enough keywords) to be at the top of the search-page results. A company may spend millions of dollars on an advertising campaign for the sake of name recognition. They then have to hope it works when someone is shopping for products they offer.

You are your brand, your personal business, your lemonade stand. You have a face that your clients can associate with your product or service, and that gives you an advantage. You can't be all things to all people, so don't even try. To be a successful brand, you cannot be "vanilla." You must take a stand, so to speak—tell people who you are. In the process, you may offend some consumers, and if you do, you have likely become a successful brand of your own.

Let's take a closer look at branding and what it takes to establish yourself as a person, as your own brand. Your company name is the first ingredient necessary to establishing a successful brand. We already discussed the importance of naming your company, but you can see how this can add to your image and your success.

As far as you, *the individual,* is concerned, everything you have experienced from childhood until now—this culmination of experiences—is the secret ingredient of your brand. Like a secret sauce, it makes you different from everyone else. This includes your demeanor, your posture, your speech patterns, your smile, your manner of dress, your communication style, your confidence, and your commitment. Determine what people like about you and why they want to work with you. Then let others know what these strengths are. Don't pretend to be something you are not. Accentuate the positive every chance you get. Consistent repetition of your character traits establishes you as a brand in the mind of your clients.

If I'm not feeling well, I call my doctor. He is the only one I call, the only one that will do. I don't start shopping around in search of a lower price. He has either intentionally or unintentionally established himself as a brand in my mind. Regardless, as a brand, he represents integrity, honesty, intelligence, sincerity, and the desire to heal me. Now my brain doesn't go through all these steps before I call him. It doesn't have to; he has proven himself. I bypass all these thoughts and just *call* him, skipping all the details in between. These details, of course, are branding.

Whether you offer a service or sell a product, you want to ensure that you never become confused with anything else on the market. In fact, it is your goal to convince the public that there is *no alternative* to you or your service or product. You want to evoke emotion in a clearly stated message, and at the same time, you want to make sure your communication is honest and truthful. Branding communicates with people's core emotions and causes them to need and want *you* above all else, because nothing else will do.

Once you have established yourself in your clients' minds, don't do anything to confuse them. In fact, if you specialize in something, it can set you apart from others. You can't be all things to all people. If you are loud and boisterous, let your personality come through. You will discover that a segment of the market wants to work with you, just as you will find that a certain number of people will choose not to.

In the mortgage industry, I am considered to be a *clean-cut professional.* If I were to get a tattoo or an earring, I would risk losing my client base because I have altered my image, and therefore, my brand. Even though outside of a little artwork, nothing has really changed, it could be enough to drive people away. In the same respect, I would appeal to a new clientele that approved of my appearance. We can be a very shallow society, making judgments of people based on how they look, but be aware, because it is the truth.

Branding is your promise to the customer or client. It is up to you to meet and exceed expectations. This is why it is so important to be consistent in how you are seen, perceived, and accepted by your community. Everything else stems from this. It is also your job and responsibility as the person behind the company—the brand—to get the job done, no matter what.

Let me give you an example of what I mean. There have been times in a mortgage transaction where I have literally not made a dime, and in fact, have actually put my own money into a transaction because that's what it took to get the job done. In my opinion, as the owner of the lemonade stand, you must do the right thing at any cost, so the client does not suffer any damages. If you have accepted work on behalf of a client, then you must do what you have to do to get the results that were promised.

Sometimes, things just go wrong. During a particularly busy time, I made a mistake in calculating some information for a client, and he took action based on the information I provided. He removed contingencies from the property he was purchasing and had already put his own home on the market. Once my mistake was discovered, my client was very upset—and therefore, so was I. I was determined that my client would not be impacted by my mistake. It cost me a fair amount of money to make sure that things were completed properly so that my client suffered as little difficulty as possible. I owned up to the error and told him I would do whatever I could to make it right, and I *did*. In the end, he was very pleased with the way things turned out, and has actually referred me to other clients. Though I didn't make a profit on his transaction, and instead actually *lost* money, the respect I earned through the experience earned me a client for life and many referrals.

As you establish your brand, understand that companies can conduct market research and fine-tune their business models and niches easier than ever before. It may be by way of professional organizations, peer groups, seminars, network organizations, or other opportunities for those with similar interests to interact. There are many forums for people to discuss their goals and desires, including chat rooms, Web groups, and social-networking sites.

Branding goes back to your core beliefs. It entails how you hire people, how you train them, how they in turn serve your client, and how they respect their positions within your company. Branding is 24/7. Prepare for it as such. Your reputation is at stake.

You don't need to spend a lot of money to establish an image for yourself, perhaps as little as a few thousand dollars, possibly even less. You can create a great Web presence for yourself that clients can visit casually, instantly, and at their leisure, as Web sites are by nature non-evasive. You can show potential clients what you stand for with sights and sounds. A Web site is an extension of you and helps lend credibility to your company.

Branding starts way ahead of the time you open your company. Remember that company that unceremoniously let you go as you approached your 50s? Well, you established yourself and your reputation while you were working there. Did you come into contact with any companies that might need the services of your new venture? If people know you and where you come from, they have little resistance hiring you when you are on your own. Growing up in a corporate environment can prepare you for the business world. Also, such experience allows you to demonstrate that even though you are on your own, you know how to get the job done. People want to hire you, so give them that chance.

That's what my father did. He established himself in the food-service industry years prior to starting his own company, and many of his clients followed. He found he could be very responsive to his clients' needs because everyone wants to talk, but very few people want to listen. *Listen* to your client so you can *learn* what is desired.

A good friend of mine named Jeff Lewis explained it to me this way: "People will pay for service and attention; in fact, they are starved for it." He used the example of trying to contact a big company in today's world. "An electronic voice tells you to dial '1' for this or '2' for that. By the time you get what you want, you don't want it anymore." He offered me one more piece of advice: "Never allow yourself to become desperate in business. If your client senses this, and you are on your last leg, then you are dead."

It can seem like every opportunity that comes your way when you are a business owner might be like your last one. You only have one chance to make a first impression, so present yourself in a way that highlights the accomplishments of both you and your company. You accomplish a lot more when you come from a position of strength. Is driving an expensive car or wearing expensive clothes an appropriate thing to do in your line of work? If you are too lavish or out of line with your industry, your prospective client will probably ask who is paying for this excessive lifestyle and may not like the answer.

You should remember that in business, you are providing a service of one kind or another and must make your client happy. Otherwise, they wouldn't need you in the first place. Go out of your way to ensure that they get more than they were originally requesting. When your name is on the door, it is up to you and no one else.

Your brand is comprised of everything you do—from the way you answer the phone to the décor of your office, from the design of your billing statements to the style of your marketing materials. Don't take a single detail for granted and remember that your future is at stake.

LEMONADE-STAND INGREDIENTS

1. What defines your brand?

2. What makes you different and able to stand head and shoulders above your competition?

3. Are you trying to be all things to all people, or instead, trying to appeal to a smaller, more specific segment of the population?

4. Are your words, appearance, and speech consistent with your message and the way you wish to be perceived by the public?

CHAPTER 8
MARKETING YOURSELF:
LEMONADE ON THE GO

What would you do if you knew you could not fail?
– **Robert H. Schuller**

We've talked about branding and the importance of marketing. Now, let's look at some actual marketing ideas. Marketing can be the most fun task you'll have in establishing your business. Let your imagination run wild. Sit down and make a list of anything and everything that seems possible. Now make a separate list of everything that seems impossible! Don't censor your ideas or edit yourself as you write; just write. Make lists of potential things you can do, observe what is currently being done in your industry, and pay particular note to the things that are not currently being done. Include coworkers, friends, and/or family members in the process. This is an excellent time to involve everyone and incorporate his or her ideas into your marketing plan. This way, you can make your inner circle an important part of your company and your ultimate success.

If you are part of a club or organization, or if you casually get together with friends, bounce ideas and concepts off one another. Charles Schwab, Dale Carnegie, and Henry Ford were all part of a brain trust. They met regularly to discuss ideas for the betterment of their individual groups. Some of the most successful, innovative thinkers of their day came together regularly to share and exchange ideas and thoughts. They found that their energy grew when they met, and so did their ability to think and create. If it worked for these brilliant minds, it can work for us as well.

HERE'S A THOUGHT

Let's put our heads together and see what we can come up with. What are your interests outside of work? What are your hobbies, clubs, passions, etc.? Don't have any, you say? Don't have time? Big mistake. You may be missing out on one of the biggest opportunities available to you: to share what you do with people who have similar interests. People like doing business with those they feel comfortable with, where there is rapport. People may not even know *why* they like you, but they just *do*. Sharing similar interests in a social setting can lead to a very successful, healthy business relationship.

Now, I'm not saying you should join an organization solely for the purpose of obtaining new clients. If you attend or join a club on false pretenses, people will see through you like glass. But if you are passionate about a particular social issue, a political candidate, or another cause, then you have the ability to work for something in which you truly believe. At the same time, you'll meet new people who share similar beliefs and values. It's amazing how quickly you can get to know people when you are working together for a common good. This creates instant credibility, and therefore establishes a relationship that might not have been created any other way. It *does* make sense.

MAKE AN IMPRESSION

When you purchase stationery, business cards, and anything else that might be indicative of your company, keep in mind that *everything you do reflects the image you want to convey*. Having a logo is another way to brand and market your company, so that when the logo is seen, people immediately think of your company.

The swoosh on a pair of running shoes instantly tells you they are made by Nike. The Golden Arches internationally represent McDonald's. A graphic artist or even your local printer can design your logo. Make sure all your contact information is included on your cards and stationery, including a daytime phone number, evening phone number (at your discretion), fax number, e-mail address, mobile number, and Web site address. All of these should be printed on your materials in an eye-pleasing and distinguishable way.

Whether you list your evening or home phone number is certainly a personal preference and depends on the type of industry in which you exist. Many people in real-estate finance give out their home numbers, and just as many don't. It's really up to you. Sometimes building a personal business means making yourself available to your clients outside of normal business hours. It can be the difference between your completing a sale or transaction and someone else completing it. In real estate, many transactions are made in the evenings and on weekends. I can't tell you the number of times I assisted in a sale that took place on a late evening or a Sunday afternoon, and as a result, grew my personal business.

Because business is often conducted outside of traditional business hours, it is a good idea to make sure that interested parties have your contact information. You never know where a lead might come from. Tom Hopkins—real-estate guru, speaker, and author—includes business cards with every single piece of mail he sends out. Hopkins once received a call from someone at a utility company. "You don't know me," the caller began, "but every month, I open and process your bill, and I've been saving your cards." Tom Hopkins sold a home to this person, and it was all due to the simple act of providing his information. This marketing activity, which took only a few seconds and cost pennies, paid for itself very handsomely.

WRITE A NEWSLETTER

Do you enjoy writing? Can you produce a monthly newsletter that can be sent either through the post office or by e-mail? This is another low-cost measure that keeps your name in the public eye. If you have compiled a list of e-mail addresses, then you can save money on paper and postage, and just send it electronically each month.

In order for a newsletter to be effective, it must be consistent. That can be said of all marketing. If you like the newsletter concept but are concerned with the time, production, or quality, there are professional companies that supply newsletters for a variety of industries. These companies allow you the ability to customize and personalize correspondence. Google "newsletters," and you should have a pretty good number of listings from which to choose. You can also go to www.elance.com and post the job you would like done along with the amount you are willing to pay. Then hire someone on a work-for-hire basis, meaning, even though he or she is writing the content, you own it.

Personally, I still prefer to send newsletters the old-fashioned way. People get so much e-mail that they delete things often before reading them. By mailing my monthly newsletter, I know that my clients regularly receive my contact information. It is my job to make it as easy as possible for people to reach me. I recently got a call from a client who wanted to refinance his home but lost my number. He knew he would be receiving my newsletter any day, so he waited for it. Once it arrived, he had my phone number and simply called me, which, in turn, paid dividends for me.

When I first opened my office, I remained in the same location for several years. When I moved my office, I paid an additional fee to the phone company so that any calls to my old number would be forwarded to my new location. I've been at my new address for 10 years, and despite announcements, monthly mailers, and business cards, people still occasionally call the old number. That's fine. I just want to make contacting me as easy as I can so I don't lose any potential clients. There are no assurances that anything we do is going to work, but the easier we make it for clients to call us instead of someone else, the more likely we are to have the best lemonade stand on the block.

THE GIFT OF GAB

Can you hold a special event? Is there something in your area of expertise that you can think of that might be informative or educational to perspective clients? Here are a few suggestions:

1. **If you are a Realtor or mortgage broker, demonstrate how first-time buyers can purchase a home with a small down-payment.** Hold a seminar locally. Send invitations to people who live in nearby apartments and tell them that in your seminar, you will show them how to purchase a home with a small down payment. Of course, you want the information to be legitimate and legal. Don't worry—there are still programs that exist today which make this a reality. In your invitation, explain that there will be food or refreshments and that prizes will be given away.

2. **Help people plan their retirement.** Isn't everyone interested in this? If you are specializing in financial planning and have the ability to help people save and plan for retirement, you can offer some very valuable assistance to them.

3. **Provide some fast and inexpensive cooking ideas.** Maybe you are opening a catering service or want to offer inexpensive and healthy premade meals. You can hold a seminar in which you show others how to do it, and at the same time, let them know how your service can help them.

We live in a time-starved culture. The service you offer might be just what someone else needs to make his or her life easier. Consider what you are already good at and enjoy doing and then think of a way that you can help others. Be careful not to offer legal or tax advice unless that is the nature of your seminar. Be sure to publicize your event. Write a press release or perhaps a public-service announcement for television. There are no guarantees that anyone will run it, but wouldn't it be a kick if a station showed it and a roomful of potential clients showed up to hear what you have to say. Don't be shy; if you don't promote yourself, no one else will.

Look for events to sponsor or cosponsor. You may have potential partners in the same industry who don't compete with what you do. For example, in real estate, I can partner with a Realtor, an escrow officer, and a title-insurance representative to put on an informative seminar.

Perhaps you can chair a committee. If you have school-aged children, consider connecting with the PTA. It can be great experience for everyone involved.

I have known Diane for 25 years. She is a successful Realtor who started working in her profession part-time. She grew her personal business via a number of ways but there are two of particular note. First, she was very involved with her kids while they were in grade school, and therefore met all the other moms to whom she eventually sold many homes. Second, her husband told everyone where he worked about his wife's career, and this led to additional clientele.

'TIS THE SEASON

The holidays offer you a perfect opportunity to show your appreciation for your clients and get your company name out there in the process. You can send holiday cards or gifts to your customers. There are a number of business specialty houses that offer inexpensive gift items that they will emboss with your company name or logo. Search the Web and see what you can find. You might consider travel alarm clocks, business-card holders, fountain pens, or umbrellas, all beautifully gift-wrapped with your personal note or card. I recently purchased 100 travel alarm clocks with my company name, phone number, and Web site address for $500. Now Waterford crystal it isn't, but it wasn't meant to be. It's just a way to say thank you.

If you have the budget or the space, a holiday party is also a great way to thank your customers for their loyalty. The party can take place at a banquet hall, a restaurant, or even in your office. You don't have to serve prime rib; it can be appetizers and beverages, but it will again show clients that you value them and that they are appreciated.

You don't have to limit yourself to the year-end holidays either. I'll bet very few company owners send cards for Valentine's Day or Independence Day, or a simple "just thinking of you" card. You can purchase software programs that allow your creativity to shine by designing your own personalized greeting cards. Believe me, they look fantastic and the personal touch is really appreciated. What's even better is when you start *receiving* cards and gifts from your clients!

You don't even have to wait for a special occasion to say hi. Send a newspaper article of interest, or even a recipe with a simple note attached: "Saw this and thought of you." Here's a novel thought: You can even pick up the phone and say, "Hello! We haven't spoken recently. How are you?"

The whole idea behind building a personal business is to be **personal**. That means taking care of your clients and their needs. You want to eliminate walls, and if possible, the miles that might separate you. There is a reason they are coming to *you*.

PARTNER AND PROMOTE

Are there noncompeting companies that you can partner with, thus allowing both of you to be introduced to new audiences? For example, I recently made arrangements at my gym to offer two free personal-training sessions to all my clients. This will make it possible for hundreds of people to take advantage of having the time with a personal trainer at no expense to them. Of course, the gym is looking for new ways to bring in potential clients. In exchange, the gym is going to feature me in an upcoming newsletter, which again introduces me to a new and separate audience from the one I already have. We *all* win!

Look in your area for noncompeting businesses or even complimentary resources. As a lender, I could partner with an escrow company, appraisers, or some other necessary service that is part of a sale or refinance transaction and offer free or discounted services to my clients. They would, in turn, open new doors for me as a lender to their clients.

DOT WHAT?

When the dot-com revolution exploded on the scene a number of years ago, many business owners thought they were done for. I was one of them. After all, the Internet preached you could purchase anything you wanted—for less money. Many of us in business thought this was the beginning of the end. It didn't matter what the industry was or what service was provided, customers were bombarded with information from companies claiming that the best way to purchase goods was on the Web.

But it wasn't long until many companies on the Web went bust. There was one particular reason why things didn't work out for quite a few of the organizations: The human element was removed. I think that many companies believed they could launch a Web site and then the rest would take care of itself. But the fact of the matter was, *it didn't.*

These sites also didn't do a very good job of distinguishing themselves from one another. They were unable to brand themselves in the mind of the public, and I think in many cases, customer service was subpar. You need a strong guarantee when you sell on the Web. Customers need to know they can trust you and that you stand behind your product or service.

There are several online bookstores, most notably Amazon.com. Yet, in spite of boasting 5 million books in their inventory, many traditional bookstores continue to do well. You have to ask yourself why. I'll give you my thoughts: I think people really like going to bookstores. There is nothing like walking into a relaxing atmosphere, looking at the new releases, turning a book over and reading the back jacket, and even skimming through a few pages.

I don't think most people go to the bookstore looking for a specific title, but instead to see what is there and what catches their eye. I love going to the bookstore near me. I could spend hours there and often do.

If a book is not in stock, it can always be ordered. By the time I order online and pay shipping and handling, I end up paying the same or more than I would have at a store. If you are ordering several books online, then you might save on shipping and handling. If there is a specific title you know that you want, then you can order online and save a trip to the store. Sites like Amazon.com are doing more to let you know about new releases and what they are about so you can get a better sense of a book before you buy. Also

Amazon.com sells many other items besides books. Their success is based on their ability to sell more than you could get at just your average bookstore. They also have categories for music, DVDs, computers, software, cameras, sporting goods, and patio and gardening items. (Patio and gardening? Who would have thought?!)

During the holiday season I often order gifts online when I know exactly what I want, as it can save me from spending my vital hours shopping. I do, however, miss the experience of going to a store and holding a product in my hand to personally evaluate its quality. But when you are pressed for time, you do the best you can with what you've got. A lot of trust goes into ordering online, and it's important that trust is earned.

A PENNY SAVED...

There is no lack of creativity when it comes to the television commercials I see for online mortgage lenders. Money is a commodity, so no one can really discount money and stay in business for very long. It's like saying, "I'll give you 90 cents in exchange for a dollar." How long can someone really stay in business like that? You are led to believe that you can actually save money because there is some secret to applying for a loan online. I'm not saying that there aren't many satisfied customers who apply online, though usually all I hear about is the discounted service.

I helped Jim purchase his home when he relocated to Los Angeles and then again when he refinanced. In fact, he referred many of his coworkers to me. When he wanted a second mortgage to do some home improvement, he called me for a rate quote. In fact, he called several times. This went on for months until he was finally ready to move forward.

When I heard from him again, the call that came, however, surprised me.

"Victor, I've got some good news, and I've got some bad news. The good news is, I'm finally ready to get my second mortgage. The bad news is, I'm going through someone else."

As I listened, I tried to filter the information that had just been fed to me as quickly as I could, not expressing disappointment, surprise, or judgment. In fact, I encouraged him to speak as long as he wished.

"I found an online company who could get the loan at the same rate you could, but the closing costs were a few dollars less. However, there is just one problem."

"Problem?" I asked. I was thinking that I was the one with the problem. He was going to use another company besides mine. "What do you mean?"

"Well," Jim continued, "they don't know how to close it."

"I don't understand what you mean," I said.

"My loan has been approved. The application is done, and all I have to do is sign some papers. But they said I needed some report for something, and they don't know what it is or how to get it."

Again I listened intently to what he had to say. This company Jim was going to is supposed to be a professional lender. If they can't tell Jim what he needs or where to get what he needs, how is the transaction ever going to close? It would have been very easy for me to tell Jim that since he'd made the decision to go to someone else, I could not help him. But as I said earlier, he had been a great referral source, and I wanted to do what I could to retain him as a client, if not for the present, then for the future.

I also have a rule in business: I will do what I can to help someone even when they are not using my services. In fact, I tell Realtors to feel free to call me if they need help with a transaction. I do not try to take their business away or sway the Realtor or the client from the lender they are working with. In fact, I do my best to help close the transaction as quickly as possible with their lender.

I do this for a few reasons. First, by helping close the transaction as quickly as possible, it helps the Realtor, the client, and my industry. Second, they remember me in the future.

I helped Jim the same way. I probed, asked a few questions, discovered what the problem was, and figured out how I could help. His question revolved around title insurance on his home. Not to be confused with homeowner's or fire insurance, the title policy issue could only be resolved by his lender, yet they didn't know what to do. I told Jim to call his lender back and explained how to properly resolve the issue.

About half an hour later, Jim called back.

"I told them what you said, and how to fix it."

"And?" I asked.

Jim laughed and replied, "They told me that it would work."

"Congratulations," I told him. "If you need anything else, just let me know."

I meant it with all sincerity too. As a result, I continue to work with Jim and receive referrals from him to this day.

LEMONADE-STAND INGREDIENTS

1. Is there a group of people with whom you would like to form your own brain trust?

2. Make a list of all the possible and impossible ideas that would serve as fun ways to market your company.

3. Choose five items in the list you just made and concentrate on the best way to incorporate them into marketing your company.

4. Decide on designs for your logos, business cards, and stationery.

5. Is there a seminar you can produce that would support your venture and be of interest to the community?

CHAPTER 9
UP CLOSE AND PERSONAL: MANNING YOUR LEMONADE STAND

Start with good people, lay out the rules...motivate them and reward them. If you do all those things effectively, you can't miss.

— **Lee Iacocca**

I've always loved watching infomercials where the owner of a new business is basking on the beaches of Hawaii, sailing the high seas on a 36-foot yacht, or living large off the coast of Santa Barbara. To quote the age-old question, "Who is minding the store?" Obviously none of these people are.

So, if *they* aren't, then *who is?* This is not a trick question. In the same respect, if you build a company with multiple locations, it is obvious that you cannot be in two places at the same time. Even if your business is fully automated, you still need people to fill orders, handle customer-service issues, as well as market and promote your company. Perhaps with the exception of selling online e-books, you are going to need help. Enter the associate or coworker.

If you exist in one of the aforementioned categories as one who wishes to live out television fantasies of rich lifestyles on exotic beaches, driving fancy sports-cars, or owning branches or corporate headquarters spanning the globe, then you are definitely going to need some manpower (or womanpower). Someone must get the job done for your clients, or soon there won't be any clients.

If this is the path you choose, then you will need to hire people to work with you. If your dream is really to be an entrepreneur, yet you want to be an absentee owner, you might want to rethink what you are doing in the first place, because you are entrusting your fate to someone else, and it is probably just a question of time before you won't have to worry about a personal business to which to return.

HIRING

Yes, this means you are going to have to hire people to work at your company. Personally, I don't care for the word, *employee.* There is something in the tone that sounds subservient. When people are referred to as employees, it sounds demeaning to me. That's just my take on it, however. I much prefer *coworker, professional,* or *associate.* I also dislike the title of *assistant.*

Many coffee bars or restaurants refer to patrons as guests. While I am discussing semantics here, I believe that there is an implied tone of respect and appreciation in the connotation of the word. When you tell someone that they are going to get a call from your assistant, it sounds like the client is not important enough to receive your personal attention. Instead, if you let them know that another professional from your office will be calling, it sounds so much better.

The way to have the best coworkers is to hire the best people. Hiring will be one of the most important, and at the same time, *challenging* tasks you will have as a business owner. Guiding and instructing new hires can be equally challenging. Before you can start looking for someone to hire, it is essential as a business owner to know exactly what you are looking for and what you want him or her to do. You need, for everyone's sake, to have a well-thought-out job description, which will serve to the benefit of all parties.

Ask yourself:

1. Is experience necessary for what you require? If it is, you will want to get the word out that you are looking for experienced people who can do the job.

2. Are you willing to train? Once you have established in your own mind what you are looking for, determine a criteria that you can fairly base a hiring decision on.

3. Ask for résumés and references. What previous work experience does the applicant have? Where have they worked before? What do their references have to say?

4. In an interview, get a sense of what kind of person you are talking to. What are his values? What is important in his life? What are his long-term goals?

In other words, how do you fit into each other's lives? Hiring the wrong person can be costly, not only in time and money, but in clients as well.

Associates are also a responsibility—*your* responsibility. You owe them as much as they owe you, that is, if you wish to build a successful foundation and infrastructure for your business. If an environment is provided where coworkers can be challenged and allowed to develop their skills, then you are also building their loyalty to you. We work in an environment where companies are always hiring away from one another, and every time you lose an associate to another company, you have lost time and money, because now you must replace him or her. Even if a professional comes to you with all the qualities you are looking for, there is still some downtime. The new hire must learn your company practices and policies, so there is always a learning curve.

Once you are confident your associates understand the company mission statement and their position, learn to trust and delegate responsibilities to them. This will aid them as they go about their daily activities. The more comfortable they become in their role, the more apt they are to trust their own decision-making. Give them as much rope as you see fit in allowing them to make decisions. I've always encouraged my associates to not be timid, but rather, *decisive*, and I let them know that I will support them in this endeavor. This is the only way they will truly ever learn.

Whenever possible, encourage your coworkers to participate in company functions, ask for their opinions, and implement their suggestions.

FIRING

As you grow your company and hire people, it is likely that no matter how hard you try, you might have to let someone go. It may not be anyone's fault; it's just one of those things that may not have worked out—the person simply was not a good fit for your company.

With respect to letting someone go, if you are not very precise in your actions in this arena, you may create some additional problems for yourself. If an associate does something flagrant, is insubordinate, uses conduct unbecoming to your company, or is excessively absent, you may have grounds for immediate termination. You will want to have a policy in place as to what is acceptable and what isn't. Make it well-known to people *before* they are hired. Consult with a labor attorney, just for your protection. We live in a day of excessive lawsuits, and you don't need to add unnecessary aggravation to your daily activity.

That's why it is so important to provide written requirements of what is expected from each person you hire and establish a process where your associate's work is reviewed regularly. You don't have to wait for a review to discuss an issue with a coworker. The best time to bring something to someone's attention is when it occurs. Be sure to keep a file on each associate you hire. Include the date of the discussion and detail exactly what happened.

You can't fire someone because you want to give the job to your nephew, and you can't fire someone because another applicant is prettier or more handsome. This is referred to as **a potential lawsuit**. You can be sued if you discriminate. If you have any questions as to what constitutes discrimination, it means not hiring someone because of their gender, race, marital status, or other class protected by law. You are entitled to ask applicants their age and date of birth, as well as for a copy of their birth certificate, because you do need to make sure they are of legal age to work. If you have any questions, refer to the many books available regarding hiring practices in the United States or speak with a labor attorney.

The people who work with you are also subject to the day-to-day affairs of their own lives away from work, and situations will arise. They have husbands, wives, kids, parents, health, and financial issues. Their problems will become your problems. As I said earlier, associates are a responsibility.

Your staff can also be a tremendous asset to you as well. Companies like Wal-Mart and Southwest Airlines grew from humble beginnings to American success stories because ownership is shared amongst everyone. Associates share in the growth and pride of the company, do their part to cut down on wasteful spending, and excel at customer service because they know they will all benefit in the long run.

Sam Walton built Wal-Mart like no other company—from the ground up and based on old-fashioned value and service. He made sure that everyone who worked at the company shared in his philosophy. People like to shop where they are treated with respect. Sam Walton took it one step further. He treated his customers like family. They are welcomed when they arrive and thanked when they leave. Today, even with Sam Walton long gone, the company still operates the way it did when he was alive, with humility and in the best interest of the shopper.

As a personal business, no matter what level of growth you strive for, you have much planning to do. You will have to *pay* people to work with you. Now that can be a scary thought. It means you will need to do research to determine comparable salaries. Check out www.salary.com for information on what the market is paying for a particular position. You can also look in the classified ads in your local paper and speak to other professionals in your industry. There are various job-placement sites online that can also be a source for salaries in your industry.

Depending on your business, you may offer a lavish salary or a meager one. Remember there are minimum hourly wages as set forth by the U.S. government. You can contact the U.S. Department of Labor for current standards on minimum wage.

You will be required to withhold federal and state income taxes from your staff as well as Social Security insurance. The IRS offers a Business Tax Kit, which includes tax guides and tax forms. It can be ordered by calling (800) 829-3676.

OSHA

The Occupational Safety and Health Administration (OSHA) was established in 1971 to prevent work-related injuries. Since its creation, work-related deaths have been cut in half, and injuries are down nearly 40%. As a business owner, you are required to supply a safe and healthy work environment. You must post an OSHA poster in your workplace, which can be obtained for free by downloading it from www.osha.gov/ or by calling (800) 321-OSHA. It is available in both English and Spanish.

OTHER THINGS TO CONSIDER

1. Benefits: medical and dental. What are the current requirements regarding your responsibility for medical coverage? Are you going to pay for all medical benefits or only some portion of them? Are you going to be open Monday through Friday? Seven days a week? 24/7? Do you need to pay overtime?

2. What does all this mean for your coworkers? Perhaps more important, what does this mean for you? Depending on company needs, be sure that your staff is willing to work holidays and weekends. Your company may be built on a unique promise that you can solve the consumer's problem any time, any day. If you can't deliver what you promise, then you have problem.

3. Do you need people to work on holidays? This goes back to your promise to do as you say you will. If that entails weekends, then you need people who can help you fulfill your obligation. You may also need to pay your staff at a higher rate on holidays, so be mindful of that.

And remember, everyone needs a vacation, even *you*! Are you going to offer one week of paid vacation for every six months an associate works for you, or are you going to have a different policy? These are the types of things you need to know yourself, so that when you hire someone there are no misunderstandings. You want to treat people with respect, so they will enjoy working with you.

On the subject of respect, I used to work for a company where management literally would walk past the *employees* (in this case, that's exactly what we were considered) without any kind of recognition. No smile, no nod of the head, no hello. In the morning, the owner and sales manager would walk down the hallway turning away from all of us, like we were dirt. At sales meetings, we salespeople were told how *stupid* we are. Hardly the morale-building of which sales legends are made! Suffice it to say, several workers made a mass exodus out the door. In fact, this was the last company I worked for before opening my own personal business. I should be grateful I was treated the way I was. Otherwise, I may never have opened my own personal business. The way I was treated there, and the way this company treated their clients overall, served as a valuable lesson to me on what **not** to do in business.

Years ago I worked for a savings and loan association that seemed to always say one thing and then do something else with respect to loan policy. This obviously affected our borrowers. During corporate meetings, the president of the savings and loan explained his grand vision and direction for the company. He told us that management was behind us 100% and promised help in marketing and easing customer-service issues. But when push came to shove, we were not backed-up by middle managers. Talking to senior management as a way of resolving conflicts took an act of God, and by the time it was granted, often any action that was allowed was usually too late; we had lost the client. There were too many layers of management, and what was being preached at the top wasn't being implemented at the bottom. I don't know if we were actually just receiving lip service from our president or if there was a true inability to implement what our company said it could do. Either way, it was a big problem. I decided to leave before I lost credibility.

If your professionals interact with the public, then it is essential that you give them the tools and the freedom to do their job. Otherwise, your company will suffer. In my business, I am fortunate; I make the decisions and I'm accountable for them. When it comes time to hiring, be sure you have a clear job description that can easily be followed. Communicate to new hires that they are responsible for their actions.

Ask yourself this question; does the person you are interviewing appear to be as passionate about helping people as you are, or is it just a job—a means to an end? I was recently at a large bookstore that had a food and coffee bar. I am usually there every Saturday and often get ignored by the person behind the counter while trying to order something to eat or drink. Of course, this begs the question: Why do I go back? I love bookstores, but usually refrain from ordering from the coffee bar, because I hate shabby service and I hate being ignored.

One particular Saturday morning, I didn't have much choice. The refrigerator at home was empty, and I was hungry. I was going to the bookstore anyway, so I thought I would just suck it up and order a coffee and a bagel. Surely, I could endure that.

Something was different that day—a new person stood behind the counter. I listened to a conversation that took place between him and an elderly woman in front of me. He took special care to make sure she was happy with her order. She complained to him about service from a previous visit, (you see, I'm not the only one who thought the service was subpar), and the fellow apologized to her, even though he had nothing to do with her experience. He asked her to let him know if everything wasn't absolutely perfect with her order. He truly cared, and his customer left with a big smile on her face, as happy as she could be. He then took my order with the same courtesy, ensuring I was also pleased with my order. He smiled and had a pleasant way about him. Now maybe he's thinking about moving up the corporate ladder, or perhaps he is honestly sincere and takes pride in what he does. Sometimes, the smallest extra touches can make a huge difference!

COMPANY MORALE

Have you considered how you are going to measure your coworkers' results regarding how they treat your clients? You certainly don't do it by insulting them (as my previous employer insulted us), but instead, by constructively teaching your associates to give your patrons the full attention they deserve.

Where do you find good hires? Ads you place in the newspapers, local colleges, Web site placement services, and professional recruiters—all of these are viable sources.

You can also talk to your current staff you work with now, as well as to friends and family. Friends like going to work where they have friends. As owner of your lemonade stand, you can help your coworkers really feel like part of the team by seeking referrals from them when you are looking to add people to your company.

Do all you can to encourage the professionals who work with you. Discuss with them how their abilities and talents have grown since they started working with you. Remind them of how much they have learned and how much progress they have made. It takes time and money to train someone. Of course, if you do a good job of hiring from the beginning, it certainly helps. You can provide opportunity, you can help educate, and you can cheerlead all you want, but you can't motivate anyone to do something they don't want to do. As W. Clement Stone said, "There is no motivation like self-motivation." Nothing is more exciting, rewarding, and fulfilling as a business owner than to be told by a client how helpful one of your associates has been. That is simply awesome!

There are many highs and lows in operating a business. You can delight yourself as the head honcho one moment and take out the garbage the next. When you have a personal business, you do what has to be done. Set an example for the people with whom you work and don't ask them to do something that you wouldn't or haven't done yourself. It's much easier to gain trust, commitment, and respect from others when they see that you are committed to your own company. I've stocked my own shelves, taken out the trash, dusted the furniture, and vacuumed the floors. Where's the glamour, you ask? It's everywhere. After all, it's my lemonade stand!

RETIRING

At some point in your career, you may choose to retire. Or you may not, if you are having fun everyday and are passionate about what you do. No matter what, you should still prepare yourself financially for retirement. This is a matter to discuss with your accountant, financial advisor, or banker. There are a number of financial instruments to consider including: IRAs, SEP-IRAs, KEOUGHS, or 401K plans, as well as defined benefit plans.

It's important to always pay yourself first, even if it is just a little. As the saying goes, "Take care of the pennies, and the dollars will take care of themselves."

Savings for retirement may also offer tax savings, another reason to speak with a financial advisor. You might encourage your coworkers to invest in their own financial plan where you, as the company owner, contribute to their retirement savings.

Planning for retirement is easy to ignore, especially as you're first getting your company off the ground. It seems like there are so many other things to spend money on, and retirement seems so far off. Take into consideration that when you put away for retirement, you have the power of *compound interest* working for you. This means that interest accrues on a daily basis. It grows based on the interest earned and accumulated from each previous day, thereby increasing your balance each day.

If you put $10 away each and every day at a rate of 10%, you would have $1 million dollars after 34 years. That's only $300 per month. Granted a 10% interest rate might seem like a high rate of return at this time, but if you remember, not too many years ago, returns of 30% or more were easily attainable. You are also not just looking to put money away in a bank. There are so many investment vehicles available today that pay significantly higher rates than savings accounts do. It may also seem like 34 years is a long time from now, but trust me, time flies (when you are having fun), and you will be so much happier when you have prepared for retirement. Granted, most of us don't add to our accounts daily, but if we did, think of the possibilities.

REWARDS

This brings us to new topic: rewarding your associates for a job well done. Money is certainly one way you can show your appreciation for the job they do. As a small company, that is easy to manage. But there are other ways to show your gratitude:

1. Offer additional time off with pay. This is a wonderful way to show your appreciation to someone for a job well done. Sure, you are paying someone who isn't there for work that isn't being done, but you are rewarding someone's contributions they have made to your company and you can bet they will continue to work hard for you.

2. Set monthly goals. Bring in pizza or some other food of their choosing and celebrate. Pizza parties are fun, relatively inexpensive, and can involve all workers at the same time. Even though this is still a work activity, it is also a social activity that allows all participants to get to know one another on a different level.

3. Throw a party to celebrate all the holidays. Bring in cookies or cupcakes or one giant cookie for everyone. Little gestures like these are important. It doesn't have to be grand or luxurious; it's truly the thought that counts.

LEMONADE-STAND INGREDIENTS

1. How many people do you want to work with you at your lemonade stand?

2. From where do you plan to hire your professionals?

3. What specific positions do you need to hire for, and what are each person's responsibilities?

4. Do you need staff Monday through Friday, on weekends, or 24/7?

5. How can you show your appreciation to your coworkers for the hard work they do?

6. How will you motivate them?

7. Do you envision yourself retiring? If so, when, and what will you do with your company at that time?

CHAPTER 10
HONEST BUSINESS:
SELLING LEMONADE WITHOUT BEING
A SALESMAN

*In a real-estate man's eye, the most expensive part of the
city is where he has a house to sell.*
– Will Rogers

"I want your business." Those four words are one of the first things I was
taught to say at the first sales seminar I attended.

"You have to ask for the business," I was told.

"Don't take no for an answer," was stressed.

"Don't leave without the order," I was directed.

"Are you the decision-maker?" I was taught to ask.

Does any of this sound familiar? If you've worked in a corporate environment for as nearly as long as I did, then some of this probably sounds
familiar. *Of course* you want the business; that's what you are there for. But
are you really impressing anyone with these stale lines, or are you aggressive-
ly annoying people until you get what you want? In my opinion, you are not
impressing anyone.

Some people like aggressiveness in sales, like it shows a real go-getter.
To me, this represents an old model of selling. I think people today are

looking for people they trust, people who will get the job done, and people with whom they feel they have a rapport, which goes back to our earlier topic on branding.

When you ask for the business, whom are you really benefiting? Your client or yourself? This takes us back to the topic of selling versus marketing. There is a stigma with selling—that the customer's interest is not being taken to heart. By nature, selling has a connotation that suggests a fast-talking, suspicious occupation where you browbeat, manipulate, and otherwise convince someone—somehow and some way—to part with his money, for your benefit, not his. If you have not established a relationship or rapport, there is not much reason for the person to trust you or, for that matter, give you anything. What have you done for the client to earn his trust?

"Don't take no for an answer." There are going to be times when you are not going to get someone's order no matter what you do. That doesn't mean you can't keep trying; "no" only means "no" for now. But at some point, however, you might see if your time is better spent elsewhere.

I always tell people to let me know if I can help them in any way, even if they are working with another lender. I know I may never be someone's primary lending source, so I tell that person to keep me as a backup. I've gotten a lot of referrals that way. I find that this approach is less threatening to someone, and therefore, they are less defensive. Oftentimes I'll compliment a Realtor on his choice of loans or lenders and let him know that I'm there to assist if he needs me. It takes the pressure off, and it's easier to establish a relationship.

"Are you the decision-maker?" How insulting a question is that? To me, it sounds like you don't want to waste your time with me unless I can directly benefit you. I find such a question to be unprofessional and uncaring and concerned only with lining the salesperson's pockets. It's the same thing when a telemarketer calls during dinner and asks if I'm the man of the house. "No," I tell them in a deep baritone voice, "I'm the woman." What kind of sales approach is *that?*

This brings us to another point: telemarketing. Personally, I am irritated every time I receive a call, especially at the office, because it takes me away from what I am doing. When I'm home, I resent the calls asking me to subscribe to the newspaper, change my long-distance carrier, or accept the free magazines. If I wanted that stuff, *I'd* call *them*. But that's just me. If you feel telemarketing is appropriate for what you do, and that you can really help people with your offer, then by all means, pursue telemarketing. I have heard of many lenders who have had incredible success with it. You won't know until you try.

I discussed the selling process with Lee Salz (lsalz@salesdodo.com). He is a sales consultant and author of *Soar Despite Your Dodo Sales Manager.* I asked him if it is difficult for someone 50 years or older who is not really experienced in sales to get started now.

"Not really," Lee replied. "Part of what I do is help people understand that they are already in sales in some way, shape, or form. If you have children, you are selling your wishes to them, or if you worked in a corporate atmosphere, you were always selling your ideas or policies to others, so indirectly, you were selling."

Lee also believes you need to be passionate about what you are doing and really *believe in it* to your core. "Business is all about trust and distinguishing yourself from your competitors. If you are a new company in business, then leverage this to your advantage. Let your clients know that they will become your priority; whereas at someplace else, they are already a known staple."

When it comes to price, all things being equal, Lee says, "It comes down to you. You need to show how you, as the company owner, bring value to the product. It can either be by doing something different or something extra or in a new way."

I then asked, "If something is less expensive elsewhere, why wouldn't the client purchase it *there*?" He explained, "If people perceive that you bring value to a transaction, they will go to you. For example, you can go to McDonald's and spend a dollar for a hamburger, or you can go to a steak house, and get one for $15. It's still a hamburger, but there is a perceived value that purchasing it at the steakhouse will make it better."

When it came time for Lee to talk about some of the sales lines I mentioned earlier, like *I want your business*, he cringed. "It's like hearing fingernails on a chalkboard. It's an old-school style of selling." Lee feels that salespeople today need to be different from the old model and *prove* that they are by distinguishing themselves to their customers in bringing value and integrity to the transaction. When it comes to telemarketing, he says that if it is done with the best interest of the potential customer at heart, then that is OK. For example, if there is something a consumer may not be aware of because it is new or different, and your intention is to help them save time or money, or make their life easier, then you are being informative. "You still shouldn't try to close a sale on the first call, but allow time to establish rapport. In the end, the customer will decide if what you have to offer has value to him or not."

COLD-CALLING

Cold-calling is different from telemarketing because *you*, the professional, are making the inquiry, not someone who knows nothing about your industry or your clients. Cold-calling is for the mutual benefit of all parties, and its purpose is to establish a long-term relationship.

Cold-calling has to be approached scientifically. In essence, you must have a plan. You need to research who or what company needs your product or services can fill, and also the best way to present yourself and your materials to them. When you cold-call, you may be intruding on someone's time, so remember to be courteous.

There is no reason you can't make an appointment when you cold-call. You may have not met the other party personally, but you can still call and ask to schedule an appointment to discuss how you may benefit one another. Of course, the other party is not obligated to meet with you but if they do, it makes the appointment more efficient.

The idea of cold-calling is to expand your client base. If you are starting from scratch, then you will have to work harder, conduct more research, make more phone calls, and send more marketing materials. You have to do whatever you have to do to get the job done. When you collect a salary, it is very easy to neglect cold-calling because of the potential that exists for rejection. Rejection is something you need to get used to when you have your own business—never take it personally.

WARM-CALLING

A warm call is different from a cold call in that the potential client has been referred to you by a mutual acquaintance. Either you were told to call someone, or someone is expecting you to call—it is the result of a referral. Warm calls can yield excellent results because barriers have been removed by the intermediary. In many respects, rapport has already been established because you are already a known commodity to each other.

My wife Anngel is a real-estate foreclosure specialist. Her results are always in the top 5% of her industry. She has done an excellent job for her clients, and that has cleared the way for her when she approaches new companies. She doesn't cold-call, she warm-calls, so people are expecting her. By that, I mean her clients tell her to call other people they know in the industry who she can help because they are so pleased with her results. Her reputation precedes her. She warns however, just because an introduction has been made, it doesn't automatically mean you have won the transaction. If anything, you must try harder to show that the recommendation was warranted in the first place.

Anngel places communication above all else when it comes to her clients. "Make sure you keep them informed at all times. When things go well, let them know. When there are problems, *especially* when there are problems, address them right away with the client so they can be dealt with immediately. Don't sugarcoat or hide anything. Work problems out together, and you will be appreciated that much more."

Whether you cold-call or warm-call, it is essential that you understand your basic strengths. I remember having a string of appointments where I knew clients were interviewing me as well as several large institutional lenders.

I knew I was going to be put to the test. I knew it because I was told so.

So, I worked on a presentation that was informative, graphic, and imaginative. I practiced my presentation skills, and then when my time arrived, I delivered the goods. I was sharp, on my game, and gave my best delivery.

I got the order from each client I visited, but not for the reason I had thought. I was given an opportunity to help people make one of the largest purchases of their lives. Over the course of the transaction, our rapport increased and I knew they were happy with the results I delivered. After the transaction was completed, I did some follow-up and asked a point-blank question:

"Why did you decide to do business with me?"

In my mind, I could hear the answer swirling from their mouths. In my imagination, I heard them tell me, "The presentation was stupendous! You must be the smartest lender in the world! No one compares to you!"

But the actual answer, to say the least, surprised me.

"My wife and I thought you were honest and could get the job done."

I was stunned. I was appreciative of their trust and their business, and to me, being honest is a given. But their answer seemed too plain and simplistic.

"What about my presentation?" I inquired.

"It was fine, but the bottom line was that we felt you were honest."

I think I was disappointed at the time, but learned a valuable lesson in the process. First, always tell the truth. Second, ask for feedback; your clients will tell you what they think. That's the best market research you can do.

I no longer worry if my presentation is flashy, but instead, ensure my message and information is clear, easily understood, and stated in everyday language. I went through a phase where I asked each client why he eventually chose me to complete his real-estate finance. The answer in each case was they felt I was honest.

I learned a lot from the questions I asked. Never underestimate the quality of honesty in what you do. I would rather lose business because I told the truth then to win it by way of a lie. If you lie, you might win a transaction. But you can be sure there is no opportunity for any type of long-term association. This applies whether it is in the form of negative word-of-mouth, complaints, or lawsuits.

A situation arose several years ago that illustrates this. A Realtor called me and asked about a property that she was selling. Due to the nature of the transaction, I told her exactly what she could and could not do with respect to finance. She informed me that she had spoken to another lender and that it would be no problem with their company. She said the escrow had to close in 30 days and therefore was going with the other lender. I stuck to my guns and told her it couldn't be done the way she wanted.

A month and a half later (remember, this was supposed to be a 30-day escrow) she called again to go over the transaction. Apparently, the first lender had erred in the information he communicated, and as a result, her transaction was still pending. Again, I restated to her what I had said before. And once more, she reported that another lender told her that he could do what she wanted.

I wished her luck and told her to feel free to call me if she needed. Another 45 days passed (remember our 30-day escrow?) and she called to inform me the property had finally closed escrow. It took 90 days to close a 30-day escrow, and two additional lenders. The last one finally concurred the only way the transaction could close was the way I suggested 90 days earlier. Since all the paperwork was already completed with this new lender, they allowed him to proceed.

He closed the transaction and made a commission. I was left with an unsaid "I told you so." Gratification still came to me in two ways. First, I was glad that I was correct, just for my own sake of mind, and didn't miss the boat in what I told her. When so many other people are saying other things, it's easy to question yourself. Second, the Realtor remembered in the future that I was the one who first knew what to do and told the truth about it.

If I'm honest from the beginning, I have established my ground rules.

Even if I don't close the loan, the client will remember that they were dealt with honestly. Obviously, in the prior example, my honesty did not make the sale for me. However, I created a lasting reputation of a person of integrity.

Some people will not use your company no matter what you do or how honest you are. How much time do you spend trying to win them over? You must realize you only have so much time in a day, and if you have to choose between someone who is buying versus another who is speculative at best, well, you probably know what you are going to do.

It is still important to develop new leads. As I said earlier, "no" only means "no" now. You never know when your competition might perform poorly and open a door for you. Loyalty is a powerful force, and to attempt to drive a wedge between people can work against you. It's always a better idea when it is the other person's idea to choose you. Then *you* are the one being sought out. This is why it's so important to keep your image fresh in people's minds.

NEVER LET THEM SEE YOU SWEAT

It is crucial, absolutely essential, that your clients never detect a sense of desperation in you. By that, I mean that you are not desperate for their money. You must always be genuine. It is understood that money is changing hands and you are earning a fee in exchange for the service you are performing or the product you are selling. If commission appears to be the only thing on which you are focusing, meaning that you are putting your needs above the clients or you are charging high fees, then ultimately, you will lose. If a client senses they are nothing more than dollar signs in your eyes, they will go elsewhere, and probably never recommend you to anyone.

As I mentioned previously, at the time of this writing, the mortgage industry is going through a major upheaval. Suffice it to say that hundreds of mortgages companies, as well as major lenders, have been forced out of business. In some cases it was due to a change in the market and the companies affected didn't adjust. In other cases, people were taken advantage of and therefore had no loyalty to the company they had first contacted.

Just as the year has seasons, business has cycles. Depending on the nature of your industry as well as daily economics, it's important to realize your lemonade stand is not always going to be busy. Some companies may tell you they are busy all the time and never experience any slow times. Maybe they do and maybe they don't. Maybe you'll be one of the lucky ones. Maybe donkeys will fly to the moon.

I don't like maybes. I want to do all I can to know what I can expect. Life is already full of enough surprises, so don't make it any harder on yourself. One of the things you can do to make life easier for yourself when you own a personal business relates back to our chapter on the business plan. If you create and stick to a budget for your business and yourself, it is easier to weather the storm, as opposed to someone who spends like crazy when times are good and then has nothing left in reserve. If you keep your business expenses in line and have a credit line tucked away for an emergency, then you can stick to your business formula. The mortgage industry is one that has had its shares of booms and busts. Business is cyclical, and as owners of lemonade stands, we have to prepare for the down cycles and look for opportunities when they occur.

COMPLACENCY

You must never take for granted the trust your clients place in you. Once you give them reason to question you, it may be impossible to establish trust again whether there were mitigating circumstances or not. Once you have earned the trust of a client, you must continue to earn it. By that, I mean it is not automatically owed to you. Complacency has a way of dulling our senses and causing distractions. It happens.

If you are taking care of your clients' needs, there is no reason for them to go anywhere else. But if you are not taking care of them as well as when they first came to you, there will be a problem. The difficulty arises for many business owners when they start taking for granted that their clients' business is guaranteed and stop working for it. If we get bored in our business and lose our vision as well as our desire to do what we do, then complacency sets in, and it can slowly but surely eat away at the infrastructure until there is no company left.

Keep your vision of your industry and your business turned toward the future. Don't rest on your laurels. An entrepreneur is successful when he is looking to stay ahead of the pack and to mold the future. Your ingenuity has gotten you where you are today. Continually strive for new innovations, for better ways of getting the job done. Brainstorm your ideas for marketing, sales, advertising, and technology, even if you are the only one at the stand squeezing the lemons. You don't need a huge staff to be successful.

If you find yourself getting bored with what you do, don't panic. Take some time and evaluate why work is no longer fun and what your initial motivation for opening your business was in the first place. You might need a vacation, some additional help in the office, or to become more innovative than you currently are. It's not an unusual occurrence. After a company has been open for a period of time, its owner can lose sight of the big picture. As entrepreneurs, we like creating things and are not as interested in the day-to-day affairs of running a business.

If you find you are stuck, remember how things were at your old job, doing what you used to do. Recall what is was like the day you were told by your former employer you and your services were no longer needed—the lousy feeling that accompanied this message and what it would be like to have to go out now and look for a new job. As an entrepreneur and the owner of your own lemonade stand, imagine how horrible it would be to have to shut down your company after all you accomplished. Feel the horrible feelings you would have if your office furniture were being repossessed, your phones yanked out, and everything removed, leaving you standing in a cold, empty office. You leave, turning around only to see a padlock on a door that once opened the door to the office of your thriving company. Feel how horrible that would feel.

Now, shake that off. Feel how excited you are in an office bustling with energy and excitement. Imagine you are setting a standard in your industry. Know you are innovating beyond your wildest dreams. If complacency sets in, know that it's only complacency, which can be conquered. Remember that you have built a lemonade stand out of true love and respect for what you do. No one else can run your stand as you do, and this world would not be the same without you. You can run your company your way. It is yours to grow and flourish. It can be this way for as long as you like. Now, doesn't that feel better? I thought so. If complacency comes back from time to time, don't panic. Just replay the above exercise in your mind until it goes away. That should do the trick.

LEMONADE-STAND INGREDIENTS

1. In what ways are you currently "selling" your ideas?

2. How do *you* prefer to be sold to?

3. For your industry, what is most appropriate: aggressive selling or low-key selling?

4. Why will the public want to do business with you?

5. How will you maintain interest in your company and avoid boredom and complacency?

CHAPTER 11
FLEXIBLE BUT FIRM: MANAGING YOUR LEMONADE STAND

The more you are willing to accept responsibility for your actions, the more credibility you will have.
  — **Brian Koslow**

I haven't received a paycheck in years. Yes, my clients have paid me, but that is completely different than being on someone's payroll. When you open your lemonade stand, you leave the world of guarantees behind.

Life as the owner of a personal business is exciting, challenging, fulfilling, and invigorating. There are also times when it is scarier than hell and can bring a few sleepless nights and a stomachache or two. What a contrast: going from the most exhilarating moments in life to those of self-doubt. You might consider the fact that you may have rocks in your head to open your own venture in the first place.

We all have a dream, a goal—our destiny. We only have so much time to attain it. How much time? Who knows, but the clock is ticking. In some cases, our hands are forced into taking action and opening a lemonade stand when we previously had no plans to, as this book covers. Still others make entrepreneurship a choice and a lifestyle.

The point is, in business as in life, things will not always be perfect just because you have made the decision to open your own company. It's easy to assume that since you no longer report to someone in an "ivory tower," you have kissed your problems goodbye and that life from that day forward will continue to be nothing but roses. Nothing could be further from the truth. Because once you are running your enterprise, whatever it may be, you inherit a whole new set of challenges and opportunities, and they all belong to *you*.

YOU ARE THE RESPONSIBLE PARTY

David, the CPA I previously mentioned, claims he has never had a bad day since he opened his own practice. I keep waiting for him to start laughing after he says that, but he never does. I've had plenty of bad days, and yet somehow, everything has managed to work out. That part still amazes me. As the owner of a business, I've won my share of battles as well as lost some, though I've won a whole lot more than I've lost—definitely more than my share. Some lemonade-stand owners are so excited about their new lives that they really believe they won't have problems in their ventures, only opportunities. Yeah, sure.

There's an old adage in business that goes "There is nothing like a good quality problem to make you feel alive." Well, when you are serving the needs of others, you will really feel "alive" a good part of the time. That's because there will always be problems, challenges, opportunities; call them what you like. There will also be many sure hits—times when you will have major successes, where you will hit it out of the park because of the challenge you undertook and the results you delivered for your clients.

When problems arise or a client is not satisfied, it will be up to you to do all you can to right the situation. It's also up to you to categorize what has happened, and then eventually, if all parties concerned were satisfied with the product or service you delivered, to label inside your own mind what has taken place. Remember, one person's problem may be something totally different to that of someone else. We all respond differently to events that happen to us. How you interpret an event will distinguish the difference between a sense of accomplishment and a feeling of failure.

This does not mean that you should sugarcoat anything that has taken place or second-guess what action you took, or in the same respect, beat yourself up about it later. You must communicate effectively with yourself about how you feel regarding the reality of events that have taken place. Don't overthink affairs that take place and how you or others were impacted as a result. Don't underestimate the effects of an incident either. See the event for what it is. What I mean by this is, if your experience with clients is good, then see it for what it is. In the same respect, if something went wrong in the way something was handled for a client, and you've done all you can to make it right, then that is all you can do. In your heart, you *know* when you have done your best.

You will have to make decisions pertaining to the needs of clients and potential clients. You are working on their behalf and have created a relationship that is supposed to be for everyone's mutual benefit. A client has placed his trust in you and you take care of his or her needs. In turn, you collect a fee for services rendered and results delivered. You have both accomplished a goal and you both have benefited.

When you first open your doors, you may start out fast and furious, at a breakneck pace, taking business and/or orders from everyone. I don't want to discourage you from this practice, but if something is outside your realm of expertise, tell your client that they will be better served going elsewhere and explain why. If you have the name of a good referral, then let your client know. By doing this you will have earned their respect and they will appreciate you. **Never, ever, EVER overpromise and then underdeliver!**

It's also easy to take on more work than you can handle. You may get so excited when the phones are ringing and people are beating a path to your door that completing a particular project takes longer than you anticipated. This can result in your missing a deadline, and the next thing you know, your client is fuming. Be upfront, explain time frames, and don't promise something will be done in a day when you know it will take a week. All you will do is agitate people. Then no matter how good a job you do, the client will not be happy.

Hopefully, we learn from our errors and mistakes. Our living is made by the results we deliver to our clients, and we want to ensure our reputation in our industry is top-notch. Remember, when you have a personal business, everything you do is geared toward assisting your client in making the decision to do business with *you*, as opposed to with someone else.

However, that being said, there will be times when *do* you want your customer to go elsewhere. That probably sounds crazy. In the beginning of your career it will be hard to turn anyone away, even when you know you should. You will worry if another sale will ever come your way, so you won't want anything to get away from you.

At some point in your career you will have a client—I guarantee it—who will be completely impossible to please. In fact, there will probably be more than one person like this. No matter how hard you try or how much you give, *something* will still be wrong. There are certain types of people who feel they know more than you or think they're supposed to distrust you. Or you'll have a customer who once had an uncle in the business who is now "advising" him on what to do. These are people who want you to give them a deal and then make it up on the next guy. And then the next guy comes along, and of course he's looking for a deal but isn't concerned because, of course, you can make it up on the next guy. Do you recognize a pattern? Before you know it, everyone is happy except you. In order for you to help others, you must make a *profit*.

You will have to learn to say "NO." Now, by that, I don't mean say it quickly or say it often, but instead, reserve it for certain people who want to rob you of your energy and give you nothing in exchange. You will find this more often occurs when you are consulting or selling your service as opposed to offering a product. However, there will be occasions when even selling a product to someone brings no satisfaction. If you turn someone away, it is nothing to feel bad about. It doesn't mean that your client is a bad person, and for that matter, neither are you. You are just not a match for each other.

Think of this discussion as shopping at a large bookstore. Many superstores carry over 100,000 books at one time, all under one roof. Some online bookstores brag of inventories that exceed 5 million books! Do you know why? Because not every book is right for every person. Similarly, the same lemonade may not be right for every client.

Jack Welch, former CEO of General Electric was quoted as saying he "concedes no markets and no customers." That's because General Electric is such a large conglomerate with many products and services. In his opinion, with all of GE's companies and various divisions, they have something for everyone.

To me, there is no shame in not always getting all the business or wanting it. There are certain people with whom you will come in contact that you will not want to deal with. When you are a personal business, you have, as we said, *special value* because of what you bring to the transaction. If you look in the mirror at the end of the day and know you did everything possible for your clients, then you can live with that.

When you speak with a potential client, sometimes you'll get the feeling that all will not be well in this transaction. You may not be able to put your finger on why you feel this way, but you know you are headed for trouble. When those times present themselves, follow this suggestion: Identify what is bothering you. Define the grey area. If you can't put your finger on what you feel is disturbing you, ask yourself a series of questions:

1. Do I feel the client will be too demanding?

2. Why do I feel this way?

3. Have I established rapport?

4. Am I being treated with respect?

5. Is my product or service valued?

6. Will I get a fair price for my contribution?

7. Will this take too much of my time?

8. Will it be worth it in the end?

9. What was the referral source and will I insult them if I turn away this client?

You create customer satisfaction because you do all you can to make a client happy. But there are limits, and as already stated, some people are never happy because they think they are supposed to get something for nothing.

Think long-term. Think about infinite possibilities and what you can do for your clients and what they can do for you. Offer to help them even if they decide to purchase a product or service from someone else. Success is not achieved through manipulation. It is attained while honestly serving the needs of your client.

ECONOMIC DECLINES

The only consistency in business is that conditions are constantly changing. This means you cannot become too comfortable with yourself or your accomplishments. One mistake businesspeople make all too often is taking victory laps after some great feat is accomplished. Sometimes they start vacationing or taking long lunches and extended weekends. Stay the course and keep doing what got you here in the first place.

I know far too many people in real estate who disappeared after some large sale was made only to find themselves in dire straits because they didn't manage their business. They stopped working, warm-calling, cold-calling, and returning phone calls. They stopped their marketing efforts; **they just stopped!** Before they knew it, the market had changed, and they found themselves starting from scratch.

You can set your watch by this: Around the middle of November each year there are a number of Realtors, as well as mortgage brokers, who start to celebrate the holidays. The last 60 days of the year turn into a giant party. It's usually the same people every year. And these are the ones who begin the new year with nothing in their business pipeline. No leads, no appointments, no clients. All they can do is *panic!* They spent too much money during the holidays...*again;* bills are due; taxes are coming up; and they have no money. It's an endless cycle for some.

Look, no matter how good a job you've done, no matter how great you think you are, we are all affected by economic conditions in one way or another. We are all touchable. Now for some, poor economic conditions may remove competition from the marketplace, and, at the same time, bring new accounts.

In certain industries, an economic decline can spark opportunities. For example, in the mortgage industry, when the economy dips, mortgage rates usually drop. That offers me, as a business owner, the ability to help my clients save money by refinancing. Consumers also traditionally purchase homes when rates are low. An illustration of this occurred after the September 11, 2001, attack on the World Trade Center. A significant downturn in the economy resulted, and there were massive layoffs. Many companies were forced out of business. However, this tragedy did not affect the housing market negatively. As horrible as this attack was, consumers still purchased and refinanced homes because market conditions caused interest rates to fall to 40-year lows.

The automobile industry flourished because of low financing. Ford, General Motors, and Chrysler were financing automobiles at 0% interest cost to the consumer in an attempt to keep the economy moving and people employed. Now in the long run, 0% interest hurts the bottom-line profits for the auto industry. Their financing unit was not making money when they financed a car, and a certain number of people who didn't want or need a new car had the incentive to purchase one anyway due to this unheard-of special financing. The auto industry sacrificed long-term profitability in their finance division in exchange for immediate cash flow. It doesn't matter if it was a good business decision or a poor one; the auto industry as a whole did what they had to do to keep their employees working and selling cars.

In contrast, remember what happened to the travel industry. Air travel, hotels, rental-car agencies, and restaurants suffered tremendous losses. The government assisted the airlines with bailout money, but it seemed like all other businesses were on their own. Some companies used their ingenuity and offered special rates on hotels and two-for-one meals at restaurants, just to get people to go out again. But it was a tough road to hoe, and obviously no one was prepared to operate in the business environment following

September 11.

When business does take a nosedive, there are things you can do to benefit and become more efficient. A competitor may have to cut back on expenses due to cash flow, and may offer you the chance to gain market share because they are distracted and pulling back. Earlier I noted that the market doesn't make you; *you make the market*. You can be successful under any circumstance, but you will have to embrace changes that are taking place and move forward, not dwell on the past. You may have to become a bit leaner yourself if you see declines in your industry, but don't cut back on advertising and marketing.

The events of September 11 are of the most extreme kind, but they are a part of life. So are earthquakes, tornadoes, and floods. As a nation we have endured terror attacks as well as water and gas shortages. They are difficult to plan for, but when they occur, your ability to be flexible and to change as circumstances present themselves is crucial. During a downturn in the market, a long-term plan is essential to survival. Consider doing the following:

1. Eliminate nonessential expenses and don't carry any more inventory than necessary.

2. Watch your staff's hours; make sure they are present when they are scheduled to be, and that overtime is not accumulating unless absolutely necessary.

3. Be sure your clients are paying as required.

4. Can you offer special pricing or long-term contracts to your clients? This may help your cash flow. At the same time, offer discounts to those who purchase. You may also have to put off capital expenditures until things turn around.

5. Determine if you can increase your advertising or marketing. Traditionally, companies cut back during difficult times and you may have the chance to increase market share because you are promoting yourself.

6. No matter what, *do not* cut service. If ever there is a time to give your

clients 150%, this is the time. If clients feel they are being cheated or receiving discounted service, you will lose.

TOUGH LOVE

Let's face it. Running a personal business can be challenging (there's that word again), but it can bring many blessings and opportunities (there's that *other* word again). To be successful, you must devote much time and commitment to running your company. If it were easy, then everyone would do it. I never promised you a rose garden. However, with each challenge, each accomplishment, you receive rewards far greater than just financial satisfaction.

Life is what we make of it. You've heard that a million times, right? Compared to the majority, only a handful of people do their homework, take a calculated risk, and open their own lemonade stand on the corner. If you are one of them, then you are a member of an elite group that took control of their lives. You will look back on a career that started at Point A and ended at Point Z with all the surprises, disappointments, and pleasures that you could have only by operating your own personal business. What a glorious way to live!

LEMONADE-STAND INGREDIENTS

1. Have you determined the work involved in completing the services you provide to clients so that you can ensure timely delivery? Do you have a backup plan or other resources in case the primary plan falls through?

2. What can you do if a client takes up too much of your company's resources or is emotionally draining?

3. Do you run a tight ship? Do you have cost-savings in place?

4. Do you have a long-term business plan in order to weather the bad times?

CHAPTER 12
BALANCING ACT: LIFE BEYOND THE LEMONADE STAND

Happiness doesn't depend on any external conditions; it is governed by our mental attitude.
— **Dale Carnegie**

A celebration is being prepared, and you are the guest of honor. You are being honored by every entrepreneur who came before you and paved the way, and for every entrepreneur who is to follow. Some friends are stopping by to wish you well. **Congratulations on your success!** You should be very, very proud. You have done something that most will never think about, let alone research, prepare, and actually attempt. You are working on a way to improve the quality of your life and that of your family, as well as the welfare of your clients.

There is still one more lesson to be learned. Of course, you will want to devote every last ounce of energy into building your personal business. You will probably want to work seven days a week, 24 hours a day, refusing to take a break for yourself and your family. But it's necessary to take that break. It's important to take a vacation, recharge your batteries, and be with those you care about.

Balance is an important part of everyone's life. Work is important, but not the most important thing in the world. As Anthony Robbins said, "Few of us come to the end of our lives and wish we had spent more time at the office."

Starting your own business is exciting and invigorating and gives you the chance to conquer challenges and build your dreams. It can make you feel vitally alive and virtually unbeatable when things are going your way.

In Western culture we all too often associate ourselves with what we do for a living. In fact, we become inseparable from our careers. Our self-esteem is at stake. If our results as businesspeople do not measure up to our expectations, or worse, if we are unemployed, we have a tendency to inter-nalize the event, believing it is a reflection of us as human beings. We feel as if we have failed and we have a giant "L" tattooed across our forehead, label-ing us "LOSERS."

I'm not exactly sure how this idea came about or why, but while our busi-nesses and ventures are a *reflection* of what we are, we are not our compa-nies. They are separate. We are separate. It should remain that way.

I know many people who believe that what they do for a living and the income they earn represents their self-worth. Therefore, if they are not paid what they are worth, they are miserable. And yet many of us have been count-ing the days until we retire since we first became employed—literally wishing our lives away! This occurs to people whether they are working for someone else or working for themselves. Don't get me wrong; I like money as much as the next guy, but it's not what I live for. My time away from the office is as important as my time there.

A SIMPLE EXERCISE

Take out a sheet of paper and make 24 lines on it, one line for each hour of the day. Fill in an activity that you would normally do during each hour. For example if you would normally sleep from 11 p.m. until 7 a.m. fill in those lines with sleep. Write down the number of hours for work, for recre-ation, to be with your family, to eat, etc. Obviously, the more lines something takes up, the more time that is spent on it. If any part of the chart is alarmingly larger than the other parts, this might serve as a wake-up call that your life is out of balance.

While you most likely enjoy the new work that you do and want to spend as much time as you can at it, remember there are other things in life. You want to be successful so you can enjoy them.

THE LONG HAUL

As caught up in your work as you might become, remember that the success you are striving to enjoy will be built over the course of years. Don't feel that if you are not living, breathing, or eating at your personal business 24/7 that you will not be successful. On the contrary, it is all this effort that will help you reap incredible rewards in the future.

For you baby boomers entering entrepreneurship, I want to offer some friendly advice that is based on my many years in business. You will be more successful if you are rested and having fun than if you are tired and run-down, wishing you were someplace else. Recognize when you are exhausted and need a break from what you are doing, and at the same time, be aware when everything you do is working perfectly. We've all had those days where everything we touch is golden, where we can do no wrong. We all have also had those days where everything we touch turns to...well, you know. These are both examples of being in the flow—whether everything is going right or everything is going wrong. When you are experiencing the high of everything in your day going exactly the way you want it to, then celebrate and keep going. There is no reason to think that anything will change.

In the same respect, if you are having a bad day, the best thing you can do is take a break from whatever it is that you are doing. Call your spouse, your significant other, your friend, or a loved one, and go to lunch or for a cup of coffee. Laugh while you are out. Don't dwell on negative subjects; find positive, memorable, enjoyable subjects to discuss. Laugh. Laugh *a lot.* Don't fight life when you find that everything is going the opposite direction. Step away from the situation; change the energy; and allow things to improve.

Dr. Wayne Dyer uses a nursery rhyme to illustrate this point. "Row, row, row your boat, gently **down** the stream." Not *up* the stream or *against* the stream. Go with the flow; ride the current. Allow life to work for you on your behalf.

APPRECIATION

Appreciation for the things we have in life—no matter how big or how small—is one of the things that is easily forgotten, especially if you've involuntarily come to this point of your life as a person over age 50 who is just starting out in business. When you focus on what's missing from your life or what is wrong, then this is all you see. You miss everything else that you *do* have. It might sound trivial, but that's why it is so important to enjoy what you do for a living and to have fun. Focus on your accomplishments and not on the lack of them.

I am a major dog lover, and my dogs have always been an extremely important part of my life. Without going into too much detail, I recently experienced the loss of my two golden retrievers, Yogi Bear and Morgan, both due to cancer and within just a few months of each other. At the same time, someone who I had worked with for 10 years was experiencing some health problems and as a result, was planning to leave my company. I was going through a very difficult time and found myself in a downward spiral.

The only way I was able to stop what was happening to me was by really taking the time to appreciate all of the wonderful people in my life. I actually sat down and started writing out everyone's name whose love and support I had received. After just a few minutes, I had four pages of names. I was amazed and grateful to all of them. Each time I felt myself falling into the deep end again, I stopped and once more gave thanks and appreciation to everyone who loved and supported me. This ultimately ended my downward spiral and brought me back up to a place of joy again.

My friend Eddie Conner is an amazing human being. He is a soul intuitive and life coach, as well as the most giving person I have ever met. He's a person who wants more for you than you want for yourself, and he has taught me a lot about honoring and cherishing oneself. He says, "When you get up in the morning and dress yourself, this is an accomplishment and something to appreciate. When you finish your breakfast and put away the dishes, this is an accomplishment and something to appreciate." I would like to add that when you go to your lemonade stand everyday, whether it is down the hall or across town, this too is an accomplishment and something to appreciate. Don't disregard the little things, but see it as a way to cherish yourself.

It's very easy to accentuate the negative aspects in life; anyone can do that. Just read a newspaper or turn on the news. You probably personally know several people who are willing to help in this regard, especially when they see you are doing something they could never fathom. Don't lose perspective on why you opened your personal business in the first place. It was to help people, to transact commerce your way, and to have fun. You will accomplish more when you focus on appreciation and having fun than you will by pushing your nose to the grindstone. See friends for lunch; go to the movies; spend time with family and friends. The happier you are, the more success you will find at your door.

ARNOLDITES

Remember when Arnold Schwarzenegger was known for his muscles and not for being governor? Well, if you are over 50 like I am, then you probably do. Back in the day when he participated in all those fitness championships, he had the physique that most men envied and most women wished their man had. I figured that no matter how many hours, or years for that matter, I spent in the gym, I would never have the body of Arnold Schwarzenegger. Boy, is my wife upset about that! I keep telling her that this is as good as it gets. But in my quest for perfection, I became an *Arnoldite*, a follower of Mr. Schwarzenegger who goes to the gym anyway, as I did, and thinks he looks better than he does. (Sorry, this is just my sense of humor.)

Working out and exercise are not just about looking good, especially when you have a lemonade stand. An exercise program helps relieve stress. It's time to yourself, gives you a chance to blow off steam, and is healthy.

Going to the gym is a very, very important appointment I keep for myself. Do I go to the gym or work out as often as I would like? No. Do I cancel appointments with my trainer? You betcha. I do the best I can. I make it a point to go when I can. It's my time and I thoroughly enjoy it.

If you don't have an exercise program yet, I suggest you start one. Not just for the sake of looking better, though that *is* a benefit, but for your mental and emotional well-being as much as anything else. As I said earlier, it is a great way to unwind, whether you lift weights, ride a bike, walk, or run on a treadmill. Go for a hike near your home or take a long walk. It all helps. It will also strengthen your body, build your immune system, and make you healthier. If you love your newfound profession, then you want to make sure you have the intestinal fortitude and the energy to get up in the morning and squeeze those lemons!

If you live near a beach and are fortunate enough to enjoy the crashing surf as a soundtrack, you can go for a daily walk to a destination of your choice. If you live by hills, a forest, or a stream, you have the opportunity to enjoy nature whether you are walking, jogging, or peddling. If you live in the city and there is a mall nearby, walk it. Go up and down the stairs and get your heart rate moving. Or stay in your living room, turn on the stereo, and just dance! Make sure you check with your doctor before beginning any kind of an exercise program to make sure you are healthy enough to do so.

FETCH, FIDO

I've already told you how much I care about dogs. You might think that the last thing you have time for now is a dog or a cat. A pet can make all the difference in the world and bring you great joy and companionship. It doesn't matter if you are married or single, have children or not, pets become a precious part of our lives and assist in our balance.

Pets also cause us to shift our focus away from ourselves and concentrate on someone else. Our dogs and cats need our assistance for food, water, and exercise. Speaking of exercise, didn't we just talk about that? I thought so. If you have a dog, go for a run together. He will love it and it will force you to get your butt out of the house! If you have a cat and take it running, please, oh, please, take a picture and send it to me. I've always wanted to see that. You get the gist of what I'm saying.

I know people who take their pets to work with them everyday. They are lemonade-stand owners, so their pets go with them. Of course, it should be appropriate and inoffensive to everyone, but wouldn't you have a ball at work if your pet was with you?

Here is another important reason for having a pet: They make us focus on the present moment, so it doesn't matter how busy or bad or great your day went. It doesn't matter if you made or lost money or if you screwed up or accomplished the impossible. All that matters is that you are spending time with them. We put our past accomplishments or setbacks where they belong, and we put off tomorrow until it arrives, leaving us exactly where we are: in the here and now—in the present moment. If we live our lives in the present using what we learned from the previous day, and look at tomorrow as a new opportunity, then we have here and now in which to live. Bless our pets.

One last note on dogs and cats: You don't have to get a puppy, especially if you are concerned about time. There are shelters as well as adoption centers throughout the country. My new golden retriever Sammy is a 5-year-old adoption dog, and I love him to death. When he came to my home, he didn't chew up my carpet or eat my furniture, and he was somewhat trained. (However, after only a few months with me, he doesn't appear as trained as he was when he first arrived!) Many older dogs are available. They make wonderful companions and are well past the teething and time-consuming stage. I would not hesitate to adopt again.

GIVING BACK

It's very exciting as the owner of a company to have the ability to contribute to important causes that help others and have also helped shape you as a person. There are many important philanthropic organizations that do exceptional work for our society. Don't forget to help them, either with your time or money.

Mark Victor Hanson, who I mentioned earlier in this book, tithes each book to a charity and donates a portion of the profits from each sale. *Chicken Soup for the Soul* has sold in excess of 100 million books, so you can imagine the impact the donations of their sales have contributed to the organizations with which they are associated.

John Paul DeJoria, cofounder of John Paul Mitchell Systems, has built a multimillion-dollar empire. Once homeless, Mr. DeJoria has always been known to support many worthwhile projects and is quoted as saying, "Success unshared is failure."

Are there organizations that do work that you believe strongly in and support? Then allow yourself the honor and pleasure of assisting them in any way you can. Donate your time, money, food, clothing, counseling, and/or coaching—whatever is valuable. There is no way to describe the joy and gratitude you will receive in return.

OUR SPIRIT

Honor whatever higher source you believe in, whatever it might be. If you don't believe in a higher power or are not sure, then be grateful for the beautiful sunrises and sunsets that return each day. Appreciate the flowers that bloom nearby and the friends and family that you have. Recognize the great and mighty seas. Our lives are not just about the work that we do and the money we make, but also about the contributions we give. It may be money, our time, or a bit of both. Our lives are not measured by how much we make, but by how much we give.

MAY THE FORCE BE WITH YOU

I truly wish you the best in your journey and hope it is a long, healthy, and prosperous one. You know things won't always be perfect. There will be some tough days ahead with difficult decisions and even more challenges. But there will also be times when you soar like an eagle, where you accomplish things you'd previously never dared to dream. That's how a personal business is; you grow as it does. You can't help but attain greatness as you go, and you will most certainly improve day by day. If you have a bad day, it will probably seem at times like things couldn't possible get any worse. When things go your way, it is the most exciting and exhilarating feeling in the world. That's all you can ask for and all that anyone could hope for. It is the best thing in the world. My sincere congratulations go out to you, and I wish you nothing but the best!

LEMONADE-STAND INGREDIENTS

1. What are the pieces of pie or components that balance your life?

2. Who are the people you want to be with when you are in flow?

3. What are the things and who are the people in your life you appreciate the most?

4. What are some organizations you can support that express your personal beliefs?

INDEX

WIN WEALTH WORTH
WITH WBUSINESS BOOKS

SALES

First 100 Days of Selling By   Jim Ryerson
ISBN: 978-0-8329-5004-9   Price: $22.95 USD

Soar Despite Your Dodo Sales Manager   By Lee B. Salz
ISBN: 978-0-8329-5009-4   Price: $19.95 USD

Great Salespeople Aren't Born, They're Hired   By Joe Miller
ISBN: 978-0-8329-5000-1   Price: $19.95 USD

Hire, Fire, & the Walking Dead   By Greg Moran
ISBN: 978-0-8329-5001-8   Price: $19.95 USD

MARKETING

What's Your BQ?   By Sandra Sellani
ISBN: 978-0-8329-5002-5   Price: $24.95 USD

Reality Sells   By Andrew Corbus and Bill Guertin
ISBN: 978-0-8329-5008-7   Price: $19.95 USD

Pain Killer Marketing   By Chris Stiehl and Henry J. DeVries
978-0-8329-5016-2   Price: $19.95 USD

How Come No One Knows About Us?   By Robert Deigh
ISBN: 978-0-8329-5017-9   Price: $24.95

ENTREPRENEURSHIP

Thriving Latina Entrepreneurs in America   By Maria de Lourdes Sobrino
ISBN: 978-0-8329-5007-0   Price: $24.95 USD

From Lifeguard to Sun King   By Robert Bell
ISBN: 978-0-8329-5014-8   Price: $19.95 USD

The Lemonade Stand on the Corner Success Story   By Victor Benoun
ISBN: 978-0-8329-5018-6   Price: $19.95

The Naked Entrepreneur   Troy Hazard and Maria Elita
ISBN: 978-0-8329-5021-6   Price: $19.95

LEADERSHIP

How to Make Money Making Movies   Tanya York
ISBN: 978-0-8329-5020-9   Price: $22.95

Why Dogs Wag Their Tails   By Sherri McArdle and Jim Ramerman
ISBN: 978-0-8329-5011-7   Price $21.95 USD

NETWORKING

The N Factor   By Adrie Reinders and Marion Freijsen
ISBN: 978-0-8329-5006-3   Price: $19.95 USD

It's Who Knows You: By Chien J. Wang
ISBN: 978-0-8329-5012-4   Price: $19.95 USD

Check out these books at your local bookstore or at www.WBusinessBooks.com

THIS BOOK DOESN'T END AT THE LAST PAGE!

We want to hear from you!

Register your book at:
www.WBusinessBooks.com to receive the latest business news and information.

You can communicate with the author or share your thoughts about this book with other members of the WBusiness community.

WBusinessBooks.com is a place where you can sharpen your skills, learn the new trends and network with other professionals.